HELPING
CHILDREN RECOVER

FROM LEARNING DISABILITIES
AND AUTISM

PATRICIA A. NORDBERG
MASTER OF SCIENCE IN SCHOOL PSYCHOLOGY

Printed and bound in the United States of America
First printing • ISBN # 1-930043-83-X
Copyright © 2010 Patricia Nordberg

HELPING
CHILDREN RECOVER

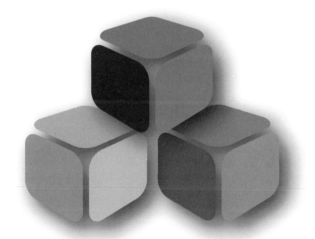

FROM LEARNING DISABILITIES
AND AUTISM

PATRICIA A. NORDBERG
MASTER OF SCIENCE IN SCHOOL PSYCHOLOGY

WWW.REACHINGFORHOPE.NET

SCOTT
COMPANY
PUBLISHING

TABLE OF CONTENTS

Preface VII

Dedication VIII

PART ONE *Autism Spectrum Disorder*

What is Autism 12

Signs of Autism 13

Causes 16

Treatment of Autism 17

FULL CIRCLE *Autism Story*

Story of Autism, Personal Experience 19

SKILLS FOR OVERCOMING AUTISM AND OTHER LEARNING DISABILITIES

The Secret of Listening 23

Building Vocabulary 24

Word Power 25

Memory 26

Reading 27

Kindness Journal 28

Late Bloomers 29

PART TWO *Interventions*

A Child Shall Lead Them 32

On the Road to Learning 41

TABLE OF CONTENTS

Discipline is Guidance, Not a Judicial Proceeding 45

Memory: That Thing I Forgot With 49

Climate of Awareness...............54

Transfer of Meaning - The Goal of Learning...............56

PART THREE *Newspaper Articles*
by Pat Nordberg

Vocabulary 62

Language, a Child's Unfolding Miracle 66

Is Your Child Ready for Kindergarten 71

Humor - Life's Oil...............77

Growing Youngsters Need Encouragement 79

Preparation Important in Developing Reading Skills 83

Tests to Help Children Prepare for Reading 88

The Development Stages of Learning...............94

Self Esteem Important to the Growing Child 97

Children and Parents Gardening Together 103

Feature Books and Stories about Pat Nordberg 107

Order Information 110

Learning Disabilities Association *of America*...............111

Notes 112

I think God saved my life for a reason. Many times, He gives me ideas. God helps me so I can help other people. That's why He wanted me to live.

Pat Nordberg

PREFACE

I tell people, at one time I was severely brain damaged. "You were!" is the usual response. I tell them, "Oh, yes. I had three aneurysms in my head when I was 31 years old. The first one broke when I had a cerebral hemorrhage and I was paralyzed on the left side, and with the other two, the doctors had to move my brain to get to the center of my head." I had to develop many unique strategies to rehabilitate my brain. Because of my personal experience, and by using these strategies, I have been able to help hundreds of children with autism, learning disabilities and behavior problems.

With this additional book, I want people to know that autism and other learning disabilities don't mean a dead end. There are things you can do to change the child's life and destiny. Many children have behavior problems because they're not learning and they're trying to get attention in other ways. I believe the key to helping children with learning disabilities and behavior problems is developed through their listening skills, vocabulary, word power, memorization and humor. Parents need to be strong and willing to take advice and work towards making their child self-sufficient and self-confident.

I think God saved my life for a reason. Many times, He gives me ideas. God helps me so I can help other people. That's why He wanted me to live.

DEDICATION

To Dr. Ralph E. White who saved my life.

Because you saved my life I've had the opportunity to help thousands of children overcome their learning disabilities. The children and I want to ask God to bless you for your knowledge, expertise and for caring.

My friend Jackie insisted that I see Dr. White. He really listened when I explained that a blood vessel had broken and flooded my brain, leaving me paralyzed on the left side. He had me at the neurosurgeon's office at 6:00 am the next morning.

Pat & Dr. Ralph E. White

Thirteen years after brain surgery, Pat attained her Master's Degree in Psychology and completed her thesis entitled: *"Exercises that Parents of Aphasic Children Can Use to Teach Their Children Self-Improvement."* Pat is a former practicing Psychologist.

HELPING
CHILDREN RECOVER

FROM LEARNING DISABILITIES
AND AUTISM

PATRICIA A. NORDBERG
MASTER OF SCIENCE IN SCHOOL PSYCHOLOGY

PART ONE
Autism Spectrum Disorder

WHAT IS AUTISM?

Autism Spectrum Disorder (ASD) is a range of complex neurodevelopment disorders characterized by social impairments, communication difficulties, and restricted, repetitive, and stereotyped patterns of behavior. Autistic disorder, sometimes called autism or classical ASD, is the most severe form of ASD, while other conditions along the spectrum include a milder form known as Asperger syndrome, the rare condition called Rett syndrome, and childhood disintegrative disorder and pervasive developmental disorder not otherwise specified (usually referred to as PDD-NOS). Although ASD varies significantly in character and severity, it occurs in all ethnic and socioeconomic groups and affects every age group. Experts estimate that three to six children out of every 1,000 will have ASD. Males are four times more like to have ASD than females.

National Institute of Mental Health

SIGNS OF AUTISM

The hallmark feature of ASD is impaired social interaction. A child's primary caregivers are usually the first to notice signs. From the start, developing infants are social beings. Early in life, they gaze at people, turn toward voices, grasp a finger, and even smile. By contrast, most children with autism seem to have tremendous difficulty learning to engage in the give-and-take of everyday human interactions. As early as infancy, a baby with ASD may be unresponsive to people or focus intently on one item to the exclusion of others for long periods of time. They may seem indifferent to other people and prefer being alone. They may resist attention or passively accept hugs and cuddling. A child with ASD may appear to develop normally and then withdraw and become indifferent to social engagement.

Children with ASD may fail to respond to their names and often avoid eye contact with other people. They have difficulty interpreting what others are thinking or feeling because they can't understand social cues, such as tone of voice or facial expressions, and don't watch other people's faces for cues about appropriate behavior. Subtle social clues such as a smile, a wave, or a grimace may have little meaning to a child with autism. They lack empathy. They lack understanding. To parents, it may seem as if their child is not connected at all. Parents who look forward to the joys of cuddling, teaching and playing with their child may feel crushed by this lack of the expected and typical attachment behavior. Research has suggested that although children with autism are attached to their parents, their expression of this attachment is unusual and difficult to read.

Patricia Nordberg

Many children with ASD engage in repetitive movements such as rocking and twirling, or in self-abusive behavior such as biting or head-banging. They also tend to start speaking later than other children and may refer to themselves by name instead of "I" or "me." Children with ASD don't now how to play interactively with other children. Some speak in a sing-song voice about a narrow range of favorite topics with little regard for the interests of the person to whom they are talking. Although not universal, it is common for people with autism to have difficulty regulating their emotions. This can take the form of "immature" behavior such as crying in class or verbal outbursts that seem inappropriate to those around them. Sometimes they may be disruptive and physically aggressive, making social relationships even more difficult. They have a tendency to "lose control" particularly when they're in a strange or overwhelming environment, or when angry or frustrated. At times, they may break things, attack others or hurt themselves. In their frustration, some bang their heads, pull their hair or bite their arms.

While it can be challenging for others to understand what children with autism are less able to say, their body language may also be difficult to understand. Facial expressions, movements, and gestures may not match what they are saying. Also their tone of voice may fail to reflect their feelings. They may use a high-pitched, sing-song, or flat, robot-like voice. Some children with relatively good language skills speak like little adults, failing to pick up on the "kid-speak" that is common in their peers. Without meaningful gestures or the language to ask for things, people with autism are less able to let others know what they need. As a result, they may simply scream or grab what they want. Until they are taught better ways to express their needs, children with autism do whatever they can to get through to others. As they grow up, they can become increasingly aware of their difficulties in understanding others and in being understood. As a result, they are at greater risk of becoming anxious or depressed.

ASD varies widely in severity and symptoms and may go unrecognized, especially in mildly affected children or when it is masked by more debilitating handicaps. Very early indicators that require evaluation by an expert include:

- no babbling or pointing by age 1
- no single words by 16 months or two-word phrases by age 2
- no response to name
- loss of language or social skills
- poor eye contact
- excessive lining up of toys or objects
- no smiling or social responsiveness

Later indicators include:

- impaired ability to make friends with peers
- impaired ability of initiate or sustain a conversation with others
- absence or impairment of imaginative and social play
- stereotyped, repetitive, or unusual use of language
- restricted patterns of interest that are abnormal in intensity or focus
- preoccupation with certain objects or subjects
- inflexible adherence to specific routines or rituals

Children with some symptoms of ASD but not enough to be diagnosed with classical autism are often diagnosed with PDD-NOS. Children with autistic behaviors but well-developed language skills are often diagnosed with Asperger syndrome. Much rarer are children who may be diagnosed with childhood disintegrative disorder, in which they develop normally and then suddenly deteriorate between the ages of 3 to 10 years and show marked autistic behaviors. Girls with autistic symptoms may have Rett syndrome, a sex-linked genetic disorder characterized by social withdrawal, regressed language skills, and hand wringing.

National Institute of Mental Health

Patricia Nordberg

CAUSES

Scientists aren't certain what causes ASD, but it's likely both genetics and environment play a role. Researchers have identified a number of genes associated with the disorder. Studies of people with ASD have found irregularities in several regions of the brain. Other studies suggest that people with ASD have abnormal levels of serotonin and other neurotransmitters in the brain. These abnormalities suggest that ASD could result from the disruption of normal brain development early in fetal development caused by defects in genes that control brain growth and that regulate how brain cells communicate with each other, possibly due to the influence of environmental factors on gene function. The theory that parental practices are responsible for ASD has long been disproved.

National Institute of Mental Health

TREATMENT OF AUTISM

There is no cure for ASD. People with ASD usually continue to need services and supports as they get older, but many are able to work successfully and live independently or within a supportive environment. Therapies and behavioral interventions are designed to remedy specific symptoms and can bring about substantial improvement. The ideal treatment plan coordinates therapies and interventions that meet the specific needs of individual children. Most health care professionals agree that the earlier the intervention, the better.

Family counseling for the parents and siblings of children with ASD often helps families cope with the particular challenges of living with a child with ASD.

Doctors may prescribe medications for treatment of specific ASD-related symptoms, such as anxiety, depression or obsessive-compulsive disorder. Medication used to treat people with attention deficit disorder can be used effectively to help decrease impulsivity and hyperactivity.

National Institute of Mental Health

FULL CIRCLE
Autism Story

STORY OF AUTISM
Personal Experience

When I worked for the school district, I was asked to talk to a young boy with autism. He didn't even want to go out to recess, if you can imagine. We had to shove him out the door, and then he walked in circles with his head down. He didn't want to go with me, either. So, I worked on humor with him from children's jokes I had collected. I had him keep a journal of humor. We worked on humor every time I talked with him.

When he was in third grade his mother asked that an adult be available every minute in the regular classroom, but he still wasn't doing anything. We developed his sense of humor, because humor teaches abstract thinking ability and develops social skills. This is an area in which these children are deficient. One joke was "What did two walls say to each other? Let's meet at the corner." (That's an elementary school joke.)

The next year in fourth grade, he was playing four square with the other kids and he was coming from P.E. laughing and talking. All the other children wanted to be around him because he had those jokes. The only reason I took one of the local newspapers was to get those two elementary school jokes that were sent in by children every day. He asked if he could have some extras. We just talked about humor and why things are funny. Humor and laughter increase the blood flow to the brain.

Another thing we did was look at cartoons in the "Funnies" and he was able to look at them in the beginning. I then cut them up in little squares and shuffled them, and he then had to put them in the right sequence. It's difficult for these children to understand social situations, but he learned by putting the squares in the right sequence. He also had to check the newspapers and add to his journal.

I was sent to another school and lost track of him. His dad is a high school science teacher and his mother, an optometrist. Last spring I called Dad and asked, "How's he doing?"

"Oh, he's doing great! He's in all regular classes except for one Resource Specialist class. He's on a track team, a swimming team, he's a Boy Scout, he goes to church every Sunday and he's got a neighborhood lawn mowing business on Saturdays!" And then dad said, "He's right here, would you like to talk to him?"

I said, "He probably doesn't remember me from third grade."
His dad said, "Oh, yes, he'll never forget you!"

I talked with him and it was like talking to a normal child. Just recently, I visited with this young man and his family in their home. I wanted to talk to him about his goals, what he wants to be when he grows up. He can change his mind 100 times if he wants, but he needs to have a goal he's working on, whether short term, long term or any term. He needs something to work towards, something to think about... "I want to do this when I grow up. So, I need to do this, and this and this, and I must, will and need to take the steps to do it." Goals make a big difference in a child's life, even if they change them many times. An example is my own son. He thought he wanted to be a lawyer. He was in the pre-law program at the University. He worked as a state life guard at Huntington Beach on weekends and holidays. One day he came home after saving many lives that day. He said, "Mother, there's no greater joy than saving a life. I'm switching to pre-med!" That was his goal and that's what he is today, a medical doctor.

Patricia Nordberg

I was anxious to hear about this young man's goals. He told me that his favorite class was ROTC, and that he also plays basketball and participates in cross country and track where he runs eight and one-half miles. He takes algebra A, language arts and science. He enjoys wearing his uniform to school once a week and his goal is to join the Marines and become an aviation mechanic. I asked him if he still had the humor journals that we worked on so many years ago. Without hesitating, he went to his room, got his journals and showed them to me. He still uses them to this day.

Journals of Humor

SKILLS FOR OVERCOMING LEARNING DISABILITIES AND AUTISM

THE SECRET OF LISTENING

A person can listen five times faster than another person can speak. So, you have free time in your mind for going off on another thought. But if you're on another thought, the teacher or speaker has gone on and you've missed information. So here's the secret: you sit in the front row and you always keep your eyes on the teacher or speaker and repeat in your mind every single word the teacher says. That fills up all the free time so you can't day dream, but it also places the information in your brain. So when you take the test, you have the information you need. I worked myself from D's and F's to all A's using this system. This isn't written anywhere except in my book, *Reaching for Hope*. I created it out of my own necessity because I couldn't pay attention. I call it the "secret" of listening because once you say "secret" to a child, they want to listen. I've taught it to thousands of children and it's worked for every one of them. Listening skills are a key element in recovering from autism and any learning disability. Even a gifted child, when he learns how to listen efficiently, learns so much more.

Patricia Nordberg

Thesaurus

BUILDING VOCABULARY

My husband was on the Seattle transfer when I first started back to school. I knew I had a language deficiency so I took a class in writing. The teacher stood up and said "I've been teaching at Stanford and University of Washington for 40 years and if everyone in this class doesn't have a thesaurus, they might as well drop out of my class right now!" Best investment I ever made. A thesaurus is a book of synonyms that would help develop my vocabulary. So now, what I do with every child I work with is to go the 99¢ Store and buy a *Roget's Thesaurus* in paperback. *Roget's* is the best. It's light weight, easy to carry and put in a backpack. I give one to every child. (I've bought so many of these thesauruses at the 99¢ Store that the manager approached me and asked what I was doing with them. He may have thought I was re-selling them.) As the child develops his vocabulary, this will help him throughout his life. It adds variety to his language and his communication skills. Think about it: we think with words and that's how we understand the thoughts of others. As the child develops his vocabulary, this will give him skills for the rest of his life. Without that thesaurus, I don't know if my vocabulary would have come back as quickly.

WORD POWER

The *Reader's Digest* magazine has a page in each issue to help increase your word usage. It's called "Word Power – Test Yourself". I recommend that exercise to everybody. They always have a section with multiple choice options with the answers on the back of the page. I've told every parent about it. It pays to increase your word power. They can have family fun at the dinner table, using the new word in as many sentences as possible, and continuing to help vocabulary development in the child.

Build up the disabled child through vocabulary. Listening skills and vocabulary are the two most important things because if they don't understand what the teacher is saying, they turn off really fast. Build up their vocabulary in any way possible.

I had to create my own strategies when I was recovering from brain surgery. I did a lot of reading. When I didn't know the meaning of a word, I looked it up because I had lost so much of my own vocabulary.

I've often had to develop strategies so I could rehabilitate my own brain. I have been able to use these same strategies to help children. Just recently I was teaching a child "nines". The little guy went from second to third grade and I said, "You have to learn the times table now". And he said, "I can't learn those 'nines' ". So I told him the secret: the answer always adds up to nine, except for 9 x 11. 9 x 9 is 81, and 8 + 1 = 9. The little guy was so excited.

MEMORY

One way to remember things is to always remember with an association because the brain uses association as a retrieval tool; a picture of any kind of association helps the brain to retrieve the information.

I was the one who won the spelling bees when I was young. After brain surgery, I couldn't remember how to spell. This is what worked for me: I got a typewriter, but a computer will work also. I taught myself to spell again. You get a visual image, look at the word, then you have to think "cat". You hit the keys and then you have another visual image on the screen or the paper, so the brain has gone through three processes every time you type a word. That's how I taught myself to spell again.

READING

I recommend the child read a lot and pay attention to what he is reading. It's so easy for the child to gloss over those words and not really grasp them in his brain. Encourage him to read slowly and honor punctuation marks because they will give him a pause.

When my son, Kris, was just a month old, I put my finger under each word of the children's book as I read to him, and left a momentary pause between each word. That little guy was reading books at two years old! He memorized and could read them back to me and could separate the word units. He was reading the *National Geographic* and *Reader's Digest* in first grade.

With reading, I think you need to capture their interest, something they might enjoy. My son Kris started out with jokes in the *Reader's Digest*. He read every one of them because he loved humor. That got him started and then he began reading the articles. He still has a fantastic sense of humor. But even if you have your child read the jokes at the end of the *Digest*, you might capture their interest with humor.

KINDNESS JOURNAL

I had a Special Day class that was totally out of control. I find these wonderful bargains: Target has those large spiral notebooks for 10-cents the third week in July every year. I gave each child one of these notebooks and they were asked to "secretly" observe other students and see if they could find something good and thoughtful and kind about someone. It was called the "Kindness Journal". They had to observe this other child doing it out on the playground or in the classroom…being helpful in some way. On the last page of the journal, they wrote their name and a kindness they did for another person. I asked the teacher to let the children read from the beginning of the Kindness Journal at the end of each day. Each child read at least one sentence, so every child in the class knew how kind that child had been. How thoughtful. It changed the entire class. Everyone was trying to get into someone's Kindness Journal. They started to do kind and thoughtful things to everyone, all the time. The whole class became kind and thoughtful.

LATE BLOOMERS

Some children have a more difficult time achieving in school. In many cases, these children are "late bloomers," who will have success in the future. Many important people have had rough beginnings, yet persevered and went on to greatness. The following are outstanding examples of "late bloomers".

1. Beethoven's music teacher said, "As a composer, he is hopeless."
2. Isaac Newton's work in the elementary school was rather poor.
3. Einstein couldn't speak until the age of 4, and he couldn't read until age 7.
4. Edison's teacher told him he was unable to learn.
5. F.W. Woolworth's employers refused to allow him to wait on customers, because he "didn't have enough sense".
6. Louisa May Alcott was told by an editor that her writings would never appeal to the public.
7. Caruso's music teacher told him that he had "no voice at all".
8. Leo Tolstoy flunked out of college.
9. Louis Pasteur was given a rating of "mediocre" in chemistry at Royal College.
10. Admiral Byrd was deemed "unfit for service" before he flew over both poles.
11. Winston Churchill failed 6th grade.
12. Walt Disney was fired by a newspaper editor because he had "no good ideas."
13. Henry Ford was evaluated as "showing no promise".
14. Fred Waring once failed to get into his high school chorus.

Patricia Nordberg

PART TWO
Interventions

INTERVENTIONS

This section of scenarios and situations was drawn from my first book, "*Reaching for Hope*". I felt this information would be of benefit to the reader as it adds expanded detail to many of the situations and examples mentioned in the previous chapters of this book. In addition, all of the information and instruction in this section applies to learning disabilities.

A CHILD SHALL LEAD THEM

Helen's Transition

A girl in a 5th grade class had died suddenly. As I drove to the school, I remembered the special letters I had received after my husband went to heaven. Many letters told me about the kind and thoughtful things he had done for them. The kind acts that I had been unaware of touched my heart.

When the children arrived we told them about Helen's transition. We immediately started brainstorming about the special ways Helen had given meaning to their lives.

"She was always nice."

"She used to help me with my work when I couldn't understand it."

"She was fun to play with."

"She was always kind to me even when others teased me."

The list of meaningful events went on and on. Many children needed hugs as they cried over the loss of their friend. Each child was given lined paper and construction paper so they could make individual sympathy cards for the family. Doing something to ease the pain of the family helped to ease their pain.

Helen's family was very poor. The teachers at the school emptied their wallets and produced $900 to help with funeral expenses. The school bus driver also loved this child and wanted to help. The teachers organized a system to take meals to the family each day. They also took clothing and other items the family needed. On the day of the funeral the teachers at nearby schools doubled their classes for a few hours to release the teachers at Helen's school. This enabled the teachers to attend the service at the Catholic Church in downtown Chino. Members of the church also helped so the child could be buried. We lost a beautiful child who had spent her life reaching out to help others. These parents had done an outstanding job of parenting all of their children.

Leukemia

A child at the Junior High was struggling academically and socially. After the evaluation, I suggested that he might need a medical examination. The medical examination revealed that he had leukemia. His mother was single, poor, and did not own a car to get him to his treatments at Children's Hospital in Orange. Leonard McGinnis, the principal of the elementary school he had attended, owned a non-running Volkswagen that he towed to a repair shop. The Nordberg Memorial Fund paid the $984 repair bill. The secretaries at his school produced enough money to buy new tires for the car. Every week, Mr. McGinnis gave the child's mother money from his own pocket to buy the gas needed for the trips to the hospital

"You Won't See Me Again"

Henry was in the Gifted and Talented Program. He had been writing notes expressing his unhappiness with his life. He felt over-burdened with responsibilities at home and thought that nobody really cared about him. Even though he seemed happy with the attention I was giving him, it didn't seem to be enough. One day as he was leaving to catch the school bus, he said to the teachers, "You won't see me again."

His teacher feared the possibility of suicide. We tried to contact his father at work. He was away from his office. The other children in the family were younger than Henry. His mother spoke only Mandarin Chinese. Our categorical services did not have a Mandarin Chinese interpreter. The school nurse contacted Loma Linda University Hospital. They located an interpreter who called his mother and explained the situation. The interpreter told Henry's mother that the teacher and school psychologist would be coming to the home immediately. Meanwhile, school personnel continued their efforts to contact his father. When they did reach him he was faced with a two-hour commute in rush hour traffic.

Even though his mother understood very little English, we tried to counsel her on how to help Henry. The children drifted in and out looking for special attention. Henry's father arrived about 7:30 PM. We counseled the parents for several hours. His parents followed through with every suggestion we gave them. They also moved closer to the father's work so he could spend more time with the children. This story had a happy ending because the parents cared enough to accept advice.

Suicide Watch

Jason came to our school with a "suicide watch" on his records. He did not interact with the other children and preferred to spend his lunch hour walking alone around the periphery of the school yard. He had catalogues for ordering violent videos which his parents purchased for him. Testing revealed a very intelligent child who chose not to work.

During counseling, I poised my pencil to write the good things about his life. He could not think of anything.

"I noticed that you are wearing clothes. That must be nice on a cold day." Number one on the list was clothes.

"Do you have food at your house?" He nodded. Food was number two on the list.

"Do you live in a house?" "Yes, but it isn't as nice as the last one."

"On the other hand you aren't living in a tent in the park and walking a block to use the public restroom and shower." Shelter was number three.

The list started slowly and then the floodgates opened. He adored his baby brother and feared his older brother. He was afraid to sleep at night because he thought his brother might kill him. They shared a room.

Jason wanted to join the Marines so he could kill people. He read books on guns and war. He watched violent videos daily. His parents really cared, but were not sure what to do. As a result of counseling, Jason was moved into the baby's room and the violent videos were removed from the home. The change has been slow. He is beginning to acquire friends. The drawing of violent pictures has stopped.

Mona Lisa's Smile

The teacher referred a child who always seemed to be unhappy. The corners of her mouth turned downward and her attitude was one of gloom and doom. Regular counseling didn't uncover anything significant. Then I remembered that the class was having a unit on famous artists. "Do you know the secret of Mona Lisa's smile?"

She leaned forward to learn the secret. (I didn't know it either so I created a story not knowing what the next sentence would be.)

"Mona was sitting there posing for Leonardo and she was bored to death. She would rather have been at the mall, visiting with her friends or even watching the neighbor children. Anything would be more fun than this. Finally Leonardo had enough of her attitude and said, "Mona, if you don't give me a smile we will be here forever."

She flashed a big smile hoping this would speed things up. He said "That's lovely Mona, but a bit too much…how about halfway between that smile and your previous down-turned mouth."

She relaxed her face and gave her half-smile.

He said, "Perfect Mona. Hold it right there honey and I'll make you famous."

Holly laughed and smiled. I told the story to the teacher. After that, when she looked unhappy he called her Mona. Remembering the story resulted in smiles and laughter.

Later, when I was on the freeway in heavy traffic I remembered Mona Lisa's smile and relaxed my face. Why should I add additional lines to my face over something I could not control. People in adjacent cars may have worried about that strange woman smiling in heavy traffic.

Journal of Humor

Most of the children referred to the school psychologist are having difficulty with learning, social skills and behavior. They are often tense and perceive themselves as failures. Before testing, I take the time to engage them in a friendly conversation sprinkled with humor. I give them a notebook and teach them how to keep a *journal of humor*. When things go wrong in their life, they are advised to look for the kernel of humor in the situation and record it in their journal. They are given an envelope filled with children's jokes to paste into the journal. When they are feeling "down," they are encouraged to open their journal and start laughing.

Humor is like oil in the machinery of life. It can release tensions, be more effective than nagging, help to develop abstract thinking ability and make life more fun. Recent research has revealed that average blood flow to the vessels increased 22% during laughter and decreased 35% during mental stress. (American College of Cardiology, Orlando, Florida)

Humor is based on such variables as an exaggeration of a known situation, a play on words or the surprise element. Thus, to appreciate the humor in a situation a child must understand his environment.

Pleasure from humor comes from the child's certainty that the situation does not exist. The joke or situation is not funny to the child who identifies too closely with it. Stupid, clumsy or aggressive themes may be too suggestive of errors the child makes in his every day life.

Adjusting for the child's age and level of development one could start with comic strips, jokes from *Boy's Life* magazine, or selected sections from the *Reader's Digest* such as "Life in These United States," "Laughter is the Best Medicine," "Toward More Picturesque Speech" or the jokes at the end of each article.

Ask the child, "Could this really happen?" or "Why is this funny?" As the child explains, he is getting practice in verbal expression that will later help him to organize his thoughts, write a clear composition and answer essay questions at school. This activity also provides an opportunity to guide his vocabulary, sentence structure and pronunciation. When you explain to the child why the situation is humorous, you are teaching him to think on an abstract level. Abstract thinking is an important dimension of general intelligence.

To understand the humor in cartoons and comic strips, it is often necessary to observe small details. Observing detail is essential for accurate understanding.

Comic strips have special codes or symbols that help one to appreciate the humor. Exclamation points or question marks above a character's head represent surprise or curiosity; horizontal lines suggest speed of movement; light bulbs illustrate understanding or a new idea. Many children need to have these symbols explained before the cartoon has meaning for them. Explaining these codes provides a lead-in opportunity to discuss the use and function of punctuation marks.

Comic strips can help to teach social awareness. When one cuts each individual square unit, shuffles them and asks the child to place them in the proper order, the child may understand that certain behavior logically follows other behavior. Children who lack social skills often do not understand this.

It is so easy to minimize tension in the home with humor. For example, when I felt the children's noise level in the garage had exceeded the sound barrier, I said, with a twinkle in my eyes, "Let's keep the noise down to a steady roar." The children laughed and lowered their voices. After a parental request, Kris said, "Mother, if I didn't know you better I would almost think you were nagging." I replied, "Oops, you caught me!" We both laughed. The significant thing was that requests were honored without tension.

A child with a sense of humor and a good self concept can laugh at his own foibles. Seeing the humorous side of a situation demonstrates his flexibility to adjust. He will also have many friends because others will enjoy being around him.

"Those who can't laugh at themselves leave the job to others."

The Negative Collector

Nathan collected negatives like they were precious pearls. If something negative happened to him, he would tell mother. Then mother would come down to the school and threaten to sue everyone within shouting distance. He may have created a few circumstances just to watch mother's performance.

The *Kindness Journal* was created for him. Each child in the room was given a large spiral notebook. On the first page they were instructed to write the date, a person's name and a sentence describing a kindness that this person had been observed doing. On the last page, going toward the center they wrote the date, a person's name and described a kindness that they had done for another person. If the journal entries met in the center, they had been as kind to others, as others had been toward them.

At the end of the day, each child in the room was allowed to read from their *Kindness Journal*. During this activity, each child who had been kind received recognition from peers. The kind acts multiplied as attitudes in the room changed.

Autism

The diagnosis from David's doctor was autism. Observation and attempts at interaction suggested that this was the correct diagnosis.

His parents requested regular classroom placement with a personal aide. Recess was a painful experience for him. He usually walked around, with his head down, avoiding eye contact or interaction with peers.

The school district asked me to counsel him. He wasn't eager to go with a stranger to another room on the campus. He resisted me until we laughed together while working on jokes and riddles. He looked forward to the jokes and asked if I had any extra ones he could have. I gave him an envelope filled with children's jokes. On occasions such as Mother's Day, I brought a group of gifts from which he could make a selection for his mother. He also chose the wrapping paper, ribbon and card. He did the wrapping with guidance. He was so proud when he had gifts to give family members on special occasions.

Sometimes when he had "verbal diarrhea," I sensed an intelligent child under this resistance. After testing, we discovered he was eligible for the Resource Specialist Program. His parents agreed to this program for a portion of the day. He flourished with the help of the Special Education teacher and his aide.

This year in 4th grade, I watched him play four-square with peers. I also observed him coming back from the exercise program laughing and talking with two other boys. The jokes had improved his social skills as he shared them with peers. His last report card had "A's" and "O's" (outstanding). At a school event, his parents expressed their appreciation. They had noticed a big change in the home environment.

The school district asked me to counsel children again next year. If I do, it will be because of children like David. Helping someone along the highway of life creates a feeling of joy and accomplishment for the helper.

Polio

Eleven-year-old Wilhelma and her parents thought she was having a bad case of the flu. One morning when she tried to get out of bed, she fell back. She tried again and fell. She could not move her legs. When her parents took her to the doctor, he gave her a shot in the back and diagnosed her condition as polio. She was moved from her home to the orthopedic hospital in Seattle where she spent the next nine months.

The first eight months she was flat on her back. Once a day her legs were moved manually by a therapist . The rest of the day her legs were anchored to the sides of the bed. She was turned over on her stomach so she could sleep at night. After eight months she was taken to the pool for water therapy. Eventually she could stand, but not walk. The children were given educational instructions, but many did not seem to take the instruction seriously.

She was allowed to go home when she could walk with crutches. Since she had skipped 2nd grade, she was with children her own age once she returned to school. Classmates requested her help in math and tried to glance at her paper during tests. She graduated cum laude from high school.

After marriage and four children, she decided to become a teacher. While raising the children and helping her husband with their farm, she finished all required classes and graduated from the university "Summa

Cum Laude." She taught school for 17 years. She also found time to teach church school on weekends. My cousin did not allow her disability to prevent her from being helpful to others.

"The marvelous richness of human experience
would lose something of rewarding joy if there
were no limitations to overcome."

Helen Keller

ON THE ROAD TO LEARNING

The *On The Road To Learning* program was piloted at a local elementary school in Southern California. It originated after Elena Lozoya, a Bilingual Speech Pathologist in the district, noticed a need that was not being addressed. One of Elena's yearly responsibilities was to conduct annual speech and language screenings for all incoming kindergarten students. While conducting these screenings, she was able to get a sneak peek at their incoming pre-academic skills as well. Elena noticed that each year, there were a small percentage of children who entered kindergarten with very limited pre-academic skills. These children had not had an opportunity to attend private or public preschool. Most of the children were from Spanish-speaking homes and thus had a difficult task ahead of them - to learn a new language and learn all the new concepts taught in kindergarten at the same time. Elena was concerned that these children began their first day of school at a disadvantage and would spend the next year just trying to "catch up" with their peers. Often, these children were referred for retention or special education at the end of the year. Neither one of these was an appropriate option in Elena's opinion. Elena knew that the families of these children wanted to help their children but often didn't know how or where to begin.

Eight years ago, Elena brought together ten Spanish-speaking families who had children between the ages of three and five. None of the children had any type of prior preschool experience. With the help of her site administrator, Elena piloted the *On The Road To Learning* program. Each month, parents received hands-on demonstrations related to a monthly academic theme. In addition, easy lessons and free take-home activities were provided to the parents. All workshops and materials were presented in the parent's primary language so that parents and children could work together in the home. The result of this pilot program was astounding. Parents from the pilot program expressed such gratitude - not only for the materials but, more importantly, for Elena taking the time to show them what and how to teach their young ones. Parents shared that many of the suggestions given by Elena were truly eye-opening. They didn't know that they could or should be teaching these skills to their children. Parents finished the pilot program feeling more confident in their teaching abilities and so proud of their children's accomplishments. The following year, the program expanded to a neighboring school with quite similar results. Administrators from other sites also expressed an interest in having this program at their schools. District level administrators played a pivotal role in helping this program expand within the district. After eight years, the *On The Road To Learning* program is now carried out at eight school sites within the district and is still provided free of cost to all participating parents.

When first developing the program, Elena had three goals in mind: to prepare young children for a successful school experience by focusing on the readiness skills that they need to know; to work with parents and young children together, helping them to share in the learning experience, and to make parents aware that they are their children's first teachers and that there is critical learning that takes place during the preschool years.

What began as a few informal meetings with parents during that first year, evolved into a complete program with eight monthly academic themes. Elena chose these themes based on critical information that was being taught in the kindergarten classrooms at her school site. Each month, parents came with their preschoolers to the local school campus and learned how to teach one of these academic themes to their child through coloring and cutting activities, home games, and community outings. The eight workshop themes were: Colors and Shapes; Numbers and Counting; Alphabet and Introduction to Phonics; Rhymes and Introduction to Reading; School Motor Skills; General Vocabulary; Listening and Following Directions and Time and Measurement. Elena felt that if children could be taught concepts related to these eight academic themes, they would be on their way to school success.

Each year, as Elena's program continued to expand and evolve, others outside the district began to hear about it. Many outsiders came to visit Elena as she conducted these parent workshops each month. They, too, were interested in finding a way to reach the needy families at their school sites. Elena decided to develop *On The Road To Learning* into a program that could be utilized by anyone. Elena worked to form her own company where she could reproduce her workshop themes into user-friendly handbooks. In each handbook, she included all of her parent lessons, reproducible masters of her activity booklets, and templates for any flashcards or games that she developed.

Word spread quickly about Elena's unique school-readiness program and soon she was being asked to provide staff development for other districts in the state of California. She began to travel throughout the country sharing the news about *On The Road To Learning* with a wide variety of audiences. Her traveling continues to this day. Some of the conferences where she has presented her program include: California Reading Association, California Teachers of English-Language, California Teachers of Bilingual Education, National Association of State Directors of Migrant Education, National Association for the Education of Young Children, and the National Even Start Association. When presenting at these state and national conferences, Elena has met and spoken with parents, instructional aides, teachers, school principals, district administrators and state directors. It seems that no matter who the target audience is, the outcome is the same. At the end of each of her presentations, the audience shares that the *On The Road To Learning* program is one of the most innovative and practical programs that they've ever encountered. After eight years, Elena's program is now being implemented in numerous public schools throughout the nation, along with *Even Start Family Literacy*, *Migrant Education* and other literacy programs. The lives of thousands of parents and children have been changed forever due to the simple idea of one public school educator. Elena considers the *On The Road To Learning* program one of her greatest lifetime achievements and certainly the most rewarding part of her career thus far.

> *"I took a child by the hand*
> *To lead her on her way:…*
> *And as I searched for better ways*
> *Her guide and help to be,*
> *I found, as we walked hand in hand,*
> *That she was leading me."*

> *Author Unknown*

DISCIPLINE IS GUIDANCE, NOT A JUDICIAL PROCEEDING

Individuals react according to their subjective appraisal of each situation. We attach meanings to our experiences and make decisions based on these meanings. Gradually we learn to evaluate the possible consequences in advance. Consequences that are directly related to the misbehavior provide better guiding lines than traditional forms of punishment that deal with the past, involve moral judgment, and express the power of a personal authority. Parents should remember that discipline is guidance, not a judicial proceeding. Today's children have a great deal of freedom and with freedom comes responsibility. The basis for democratic living within the home, and in society, is mutual respect and shared responsibility. Yet, our children cannot become responsible until responsibility is given to them. Logical consequences as a disciplinary method teaches the child to accept the responsibility for his own behavior.

Fundamental motivation

Many psychologists believe that the need to belong and to be accepted is the basic human motivation. Ideally, our children soon discover that contributing to the welfare of others is the best way to gain and maintain acceptance. Security comes from knowing one is worthwhile and has a place within the group. Teaching a child what he can do for, and with, his fellow man helps him to fulfill this basic human need.

When the child feels more secure within the group he will show more concern with enhancing the welfare of others. Conversely, a child who has always persuaded his parents to cater to his demands interprets the behavior of others in light of whether it will serve his demands. A child such as this only sees cooperation and sharing as interference.

 Patricia Nordberg

Eventually he ceases to cooperate or participate.

"We can find immediate goals behind every misbehavior. All misbehavior is the result of a child's mistaken assumption about the way he can find a place and gain status." (Dreikurs) When a parent is unaware of the meaning of the behavior, he falls for the "non-conscious scheme" and reinforces the behavior. Varying one's response and reacting in a manner different from what the child expects is often very effective.

In his book *Logical Consequences: a New Approach to Discipline*, Dreikurs identifies the three goals of misbehavior as: attention-getting, struggle for power and revenge.

Using disability as an excuse

Often sibling relationships are a greater influence on personality development than the child's relationship to his parents. For example, where one child succeeds, the other may give up or attempt to shine in another area. The problems develop when a child feels he can never compete through constructive channels. Minimizing the attention given for misbehavior and maximizing the attention given for constructive behavior helps the child to find his place. A child with high self esteem will not need constant testimonials, but will find fulfillment through the cooperative activity itself.

"Once the battle has been joined, the child has already won it." (Dreikurs) Parental disinvolvement is the first requirement in a power struggle. There is not much point to a power struggle when the power is not contested or does not have an audience. Parents talk too much. If the child knew the consequences before he committed the act, the parent should follow through with the minimum of conversation. The child has made his choice and must experience the consequence. Preaching, advising, explaining and "I told you so" comments are useless. Too much talking makes the child "parent-deaf."

The child bent on revenge feels that the only way he can achieve recognition is by provoking hostility. He feels he has been pushed around by adults - and he may be right! He does not seem to realize that the kind of treatment he receives is the result of his behavior. Parents must draw this child into a constructive partnership so that he can gain status and recognition through useful behavior.

Inadequacy or assumed disability is perhaps the most extreme form of discouragement. A discouraged child should be given recognition for what he can do with the accent placed on his assets. Encouragement is the specific need. Special training in his deficits will help to develop functions that should have been developed earlier. One must guard against overprotection, for this robs the child of experiencing his own strength. A dependent child is a handicapped child.

How not to fight

A logical consequence is defined as the natural result of an ill-advised act. When the consequence is unpleasant, the child may avoid the act in the future unless there is some benefit in its continuation. For the consequence to be effective it must be experienced by the child as logical in nature. A logical consequence gives the child a choice of whether or not he wants to repeat the act. Remember! The consequence must be relevant to the misdeed and something the parent can follow through on. When following through the tone of voice should be friendly. A "this will teach you a lesson" attitude turns a consequence into a punishment.

Children who are exposed to punishment usually need continued punishment for any type of cooperation. "Kindness expresses respect for the child and firmness evokes respect from the child." (Dreikurs) When traditional forms of punishment are replaced by logical or natural consequences the child responds to the needs of reality and not to the power of the adult.

Two-thirds of *Logical Consequences: a New Approach to Discipline* is devoted to practical examples: home situations involving young children, elementary school situations and logical consequences with adolescents. In each example the author describes a situation in detail. He then relates how the situation was handled. If the situation was handled correctly he tells why this is the correct method. If the situation was handled incorrectly he tells why this method was incorrect. These practical examples help the parent to understand how to apply the principles inherent in logical consequences.

"In quietness and in confidence shall be your strength."

Isaiah 30:15

MEMORY: THAT THING I FORGOT WITH...

The child who made this statement did not realize that "forgotten" material is really not gone. The information was either not placed into his long-term memory store or he was using inadequate strategies to retrieve it.

In the August, 1971 issue of *Scientific American* (p. 83) Atkinson and Shiffrin stated, "All phases of memory are assumed to consist of small units of information that are associatively related ... Information from the environment is accepted and processed by the various sensory systems and is entered into the short-term store. Rehearsal can be shown not only to maintain information in the short-term storage but also to transfer from the short-term store to the long-term one." Their research data confirmed "that long-term store retrieval closely parallels the number of rehearsals given an item during presentation." The retrieval of information from the long-term store requires strategy and selection. One must first find access to a small subset of information that has the desired image. When the information has been placed in the long-term memory with an association, the brain can later use this association as a probe to more quickly retrieve the desired information. Their research seemed to point to the assumption that forgetting is a result of inadequate selection of probe information.

Attentive listening and/or close observation is essential to a good memory. Children who are easily distracted or find it difficult to concentrate often miss the first part of an instruction because they are slow in preparing themselves to listen. Words such as *ready*, *listen* or *next* can be used with visual cues or touching before giving information or instructions. Waiting a few seconds and a slower presentation helps to facilitate recall. Teachers of learning disabled children use all sensory modalities to reinforce the retention of concepts. For example, when teaching reading by the "open court" method the teacher combines an auditory stimulus with visual associations to help the child remember. This program also introduces humor - another helpful aid to memory.

Two processes

Recognition of the familiar and remembering appear to be two separate processes, although the latter may be an elaboration of the first. Learning disabilities can occur at either level. For instance, a child who does not visually recognize words cannot read. If a child can recognize words but not revisualize them he can read but not write. Another child might understand a word when it is spoken but not be able to recall it for his communication needs. This latter child may try to participate in classroom discussions but forget what he planned to say.

When discussing memory it is not easy to evolve a frame of reference without including imagery. "Imaging" is a mental process in which verbal information is remembered through visual images. In revisualizing a person recalls how the experience actually appeared visually. Reauditorizing involves recalling the sounds that made up a part of the experience.

Teachers have long known that the picture-evoking value of words is an important determiner in ease of learning. Children learn to read words for which they can form a thought picture (airplane) more easily than words such as *either*, *here* or *was*. Imagery is used as an aid to listening memory in the spelling technique of thinking of a word as being on a large billboard.

Teaching a child how to revisualize letters and words helps him to write and spell properly. Visual cues and auditory and kinesthetic activities are helpful in getting responses from children with revisualization deficits. The child who spells words aloud while writing them, reveals a need for audition to serve as a mediating process. Practicing spelling words on a typewriter gives the brain many cues. The child looks closely at a word, actively thinks about the sequencing of each individual letter within the word as he types, then looks at his reproduction on the typed page. Even a very young child using the one finger "hunt and peck" system has imprinted his brain with two visual images, and with conscious thought about the spelling of the word. His memory can be helped even further when associations such as are found in "word families" are introduced. (make, cake, take, lake) One child who was having extreme difficulty with the word "friend" remembered how to spell it after it was pointed out to her that the last half of the word was spelled "end."

Patterns are also helpful memory clues. Multiplication by nine is easily remembered after the pattern is pointed out to the child:

$9X1 = 09$
$9X2 = 18$
$9X3 = 27$
$9X4 = 36$
$9X5 = 45$
$9X6 = 54$
$9X7 = 63$
$9X8 = 72$
$9X9 = 81$

On the left hand side of the column one reads downward: 0, 1, 2, 3, 4, 5, 6, 7, 8 and on the right side one reads: 9, 8, 7 6, 5, 4, 3, 2, 1. Teach your child to look for patterns, clues and associations in things he needs to remember.

When helping a child to reauditorize it is necessary for the auditory stimulus to be carefully tuned with the experience. Structure the environment so that the child can take an active part in starting or stopping the auditory stimulus. The key is to develop an auditory awareness. Since auditory memory is critical for language development the writer refers you to Selma Herr's *Perceptual Communication Skills*. This book has 264 activities for developing auditory awareness and insight at all age levels.

The following research findings may suggest new methods that you can use to help your children remember:

Pleasant items or experiences are more readily recalled than unpleasant ones. Memories that enhance self-esteem are more easily recalled.

Interspersed study periods produce more rapid memorization than do massed sessions. This suggests that some sort of consolidation occurs after practice.

Meaningful material is easier to memorize than nonmeaningful material and once learned, it is retained longer.

Things important to remember are remembered better than things that do not make any difference. ("importance" is defined subjectively)

General social attitudes influence memory.

When subjects learned a series of paired associates, repeated exposure was not necessary for mastery.

Material previously learned and "forgotten" can be relearned with less effort than it took to learn it in the first place.

Other things being equal, the better perceived and learned, according to the laws of perception and learning, the longer and-or more accurately the material will be remembered.

Events that stand in isolation are much better remembered than those followed by other events of similar nature, and somewhat better remembered than events preceded by similar ones.

Remembered material undergoes systematic and meaningful changes reflecting, as in perception, tendencies to select, organize, and interpret.

With verbal materials, reading coupled with active recitation leads to much more efficient memorizing than reading only. Similar findings hold for memorizing meaningful passages, spelling and arithmetic. However, the advantage of recitation diminishes as the material becomes more meaningful and or as the response involves comprehension.

The beginning and the end of a series of items are memorized more quickly than the items in the middle (the "serial position effect")

Sleep immediately following learning results in more retention (82 to 86 per cent) than when the subject stays awake after learning.

"As a psychoneurological function, memory is all encompassing, being entailed in essentially all mental functions."

Myklebust and Johnson

CLIMATE OF AWARENESS

Children are particularly sensitive to a social climate. A child develops feelings that he is liked, wanted, accepted and able through the experience of being treated as though he were so. When a child has a good self-concept, he is free to devote his energies to behavior that is positive and constructive.

Parents and teachers can structure a climate for positive feedback by teaching children to watch for positive behavior in others. A very effective program was developed by Robert Slagle in Tennessee.

Children in the classroom were divided into small groups to play the "Peanut Pals" game. (In junior high it was called "Secret Agent.")

Each child drew a piece of paper with the secret pal's name on it. Throughout the day they were supposed to be particularly nice to their "Peanut Pal." At the end of the day a "pow wow" meeting was held. Going around the circle, each child said, "What I liked about myself today was...." Every other child said to the first child: "What I liked about you today was..." Then the child being discussed said, "I think _____ was my Peanut Pal because..." The child related specific behavior that caused him to believe this child was his Peanut Pal. The most important rule of the game: negative words cannot be used.

Many of the children became considerate toward all others so their peers would have a more difficult time guessing who their Peanut Pal was. As thoughtfulness became a habit pattern with the children, they blossomed. This exercise helped the child to become aware of his own behavior and how his behavior affects others.

The same general format can be used in the home environment to develop a climate of awareness. If the family is small, parents or neighborhood children can be a part of the group.

In the Tennessee program the "pow wow" meetings became the most significant part of the day for the children. How comforting for a child to go to bed after having been reinforced for the positive things he did during the day. He feels better about himself and is then able to reach out and help others feel better about themselves.

Although the above activity can be adapted to all age levels, older children sometimes need more concrete experiences to heighten their awareness. An activity suggested by Dr. Robert Vallett has been very successful. He asks the child to print his name in large letters in the center of a sheet of paper. In one corner of the paper he writes the name of the person who has been a great influence on his life. In another corner he writes and notes the year that was the best; in the opposite corner the year that was the worst. In the last corner, his goal for his life.

The entire class, or members of the household, view what each has written on his paper.

In the classroom, the child pairs with one other person; at home the group can include the entire family. The ways in which another person has influenced his life is explained by the child. The child relates why a certain year was the best and why another year was the worst. He talks in depth about the goal he has established for his life.

In a classroom situation, a teacher may ask for volunteers to tell about meaningful experiences that have changed their lives. As the participants relate the significant behavior of others, they become more aware of how their behavior influences the lives of those around them. When goals are discussed, children learn to see themselves as part of the ongoing growth process. Understanding this process of becoming in others may be a first step in understanding and accepting that process in oneself.

"If one life shines, the next life to it must catch the light.
It is the infection of excellence."

A.D.T. Whitney

Patricia Nordberg

TRANSFER OF MEANING – THE GOAL OF LEARNING

Skillful listening and communication do not "just happen." If half of all the mental growth a child will acquire is possessed by about the age of four, it would seem that we are restricting the development of our children if we wait until they start school before teaching them how to listen.

Listening is more than hearing and attending. It is "the process by which spoken language is converted to meaning in the mind." Listening is the first language skill to appear. There is a progressive sequence of development in which children listen before they speak, speak before they read, and read before they write. Sara Lundsteen, author of *Children Learn to Communicate* (1972), wrote that "reading may depend so completely upon listening that it appears to be a special extension of listening...Since reading is normally superimposed on a listening foundation, the ability to listen seems to set limits on the ability to read... Listening also provides the key to unlocking progress in any other area related to language and that includes science, history, math -- the whole of education."

While in school, children spend more than one-half of the day listening. For a college student it may be as high as 90 per cent. Efficient listening might include practice in concentration and attention, learning how to filter out noises that cover up the message, dealing with auditory fatigue, and using past background to aid in anticipating the message.

Distortions occur

Listeners frequently receive what they expect to receive rather than what the message-giver intended. The first distortion is the intrusion of one's attitude that selects and filters the information. A second possible distortion is attributing a motive to the speaker. A third may surface in organizing the information. A fourth distortion occurs when the listener thinks about the response he will give as soon as the speaker is finished.

Supposedly, the proficient listener organizes, gets meaning, and thinks beyond the listening. Lundsteen labels the ten steps as: (1) hear, (2) hold in memory, (3) attend, (4) form images, (5) search memory store, (6) compare, (7) test cues, (8) recode, (9) get meaning, and (10) intellectualize. Since we take on only the language demanded by the task, listening represents sampling and hypothesis testing. Children increase their ability to judge from samples as they grow older and have more experiences with which to relate the message. A listener brings his background of facts, ideas, rules, principles, attitudes, sets, values, beliefs, and language base to every listening encounter. "If a listener has no background specific to the message, he can accomplish intake physiologically but not listen." (Lundsteen, 1972)

The transfer of meaning is the goal of listening. Meanings change with time, context and the user. For example: each person-to-person communication also involves all the qualifiers of language (tone of voice, tempo, etc.), the kinetics of non-vocal bodily movement (hand gestures, raised eyebrows, shoulder shrugs), touch, and most important, feedback. Parents should observe all nonverbal channels used by their children. They are observing yours.

Children should be encouraged to think about the experiences that relate to the message and to ask questions: *What do you mean?* or *What time?* or *Where?* Only when a listener's experiences bring meaning to the verbal symbols is he in a position to make appropriate responses. This is one of the reasons why a variety of experiences is necessary for a child's intellectual development.

Accurate hearing

Accurate hearing is a prerequisite to listening. Auditory acuity refers to reception of sound waves and defines the efficiency of the hearing organs. Some specialists believe that five to ten percent of our children have auditory acuity handicaps. When tonsil and adenoid infections cause temporary hearing loss, the child may lose valuable opportunities for learning auditory discriminations needed for learning to read. Observe: does your child lean forward to hear, speak too loudly or too softly, have trouble pronouncing words, have difficulty with rhyming words, or discriminating similar sounds from one another. Auditory acuity may set the limits within which auditory discrimination can operate.

Auditory discrimination refers to distinction of sounds. This acquired skill frequently matures as late as the end of age eight. A child needs fine discriminations to hear words as made up of initial, middle, and final sounds and to separate sounds that distinguish one word from another.

When we talk, words run together. We hear bursts of sound to which we make connections for processing. To a child having trouble hearing the separation of words, a sentence may sound like "Slurvian." For example:

1. Turnip outs fir ply. (Turn about is fair play.)

2. A nap a lad hay keys a dock tray weigh. (An apple a day keeps the doctor away.)

3. Asher wait a bulb ounces. (That's the way the ball bounces.)

Talking slowly, with a momentary pause between words helps to insure understanding. Think for a moment. If you had taken several classes in conversational Spanish, would you be able to understand every word your Spanish-speaking friend said while she was speaking at her normal rate?

Children can be helped to assume responsibility for the control of their attention. Discuss the importance of efficient listening and bring it to the level of their consciousness. Explain that a person can listen five times as fast as another person can talk. This leaves a span of free time for daydreaming. The daydream can last from a few moments to a few minutes. If it lasts a few minutes the listener has lost a great deal of information. Suggest to your child that when he is listening to someone speak to always focus his eyes on the speaker's mouth or eyes. While he is doing this he will have time to silently rehearse in his mind (not with his lips) everything the speaker says. Rehearsing helps to place the information in his memory and does not leave time for distractibility.

There are many activities designed to develop auditory awareness and insight in children. Selma Herr's *Perceptual Communication Skills* includes most of them: listening for details, following directions, drawing conclusions, learning to use judgment, learning to remember, discriminative listening and memory development.

The Teacher's Handbook is easy to follow and has been used successfully by many parents. The handbook contains directions for all programs from preschool through high school ($7.50). There are three corresponding workbooks for the different levels ($1.40 each). Program one: preschool through grades 1, 2, 3; Program two: Grades 4, 5, 6; and Program three: junior high, senior high, adults.

Children enjoy these activities so much that many teachers have found it useful to save them for rewards. Parents can purchase them at any teacher supply store or by writing to the publisher: Instructional Materials and Equipment, 1520 Cotner Avenue, Los Angeles, CA 90025.

As a helpful parent, remember to praise and otherwise reinforce your child for his efforts and successes. If you keep teaching sessions short and fun, and stop while interest is high, you and your children will cherish these moments together.

> *"Whatever you can do, or dream you can, begin it.*
> *Boldness has genius, power and magic in it."*
>
> *Goethe*

PART THREE

Newspaper Articles

by Pat Nordberg

When I was turned down at Northwestern to work on my doctorate because I was too old, I joined the Association for Children with Learning Disabilties in Barrington, and through them I wrote a weekly newspaper column that was distributed to all the Chicago suburbs telling parents how to develop potential in their children. Parents, teachers and principals were coming in for extra copies.

As these articles deal with all phases of child development and represents a phase of my career, I decided to include them for the reader's referral and interest.

by Pat Nordberg

VOCABULARY

Our National Resource

High achievers in almost any activity - from student to corporation executive - score high in vocabulary.

An undeveloped vocabulary is often one of the contributing reasons for deficiency in reading ability. Comprehension is the goal of reading. How can a child understand the meaning of a sentence when he does not know the meaning of some words within it? During individual testing, a student will often ask the meaning of commonly used words. This same child did not always understand the teacher in the classroom, but feared laughter from his peers if he asked the meaning of a word.

Vocabulary Development

The natural way to develop a vocabulary is to widen interests. A curious six to ten-year-old child learns the meaning of approximately 5000 words a year. Parents can keep the momentum of curiosity going by encouraging hobbies and activities that enrich the child's word collection.

For the young child, the *Little Golden Dictionary* presents over one thousand words with simple definitions and a colorful, descriptive picture beside each word. For older children and adults, Johnson O'Connor's *Vocabulary Builder* and the *Reader's Digest* hard cover book *How to Increase Your Word Power* are very helpful. *How to Increase Your Word Power* stresses the importance of learning basic prefixes, suffixes and root words as a means of unlocking the meaning of previously unencountered words. The book also has word games and quizzes to help the reader retain the information.

Patricia Nordberg

Each month the *Reader's Digest* magazine has an article entitled "It Pays to Enrich Your Word Power." Twenty words are listed with four possible meanings to choose from. The answers are on the back of the page, often with a sentence using the word correctly. One could borrow back issues from a friend. Since the articles are timeless the date of issue is unimportant.

The family could take one word a day for study. After the meaning of the word is thoroughly discussed, the parents could make a game of using that word as much as possible in the conversation. After twenty days have passed one could use the following ten days for a review of all the new words learned that month. There are multiple opportunities for humor and discussion as each family member tries to use the new words creatively.

Every child old enough to use a dictionary should have his own copy of *Roget's College Thesaurus* in dictionary form. Thesaurus is pronounced phonetically: the-sau-rus. Don't let the word "college" in the title concern you. Children from the 6th grade on have used this book effectively. Each word is listed in alphabetical order followed by all the other words that have the same meaning. There are no lengthy definitions - only synonyms. It is a valuable tool for any child who has to write a composition.

Writing

Writing helps a child organize his thoughts. The famous semanticist S.I. Hayakawa believes that "Learning to write is learning to think." Encouraging a child to keep a diary of his feelings about daily events serves both a semantic and psychological purpose. Your son might wish to refer to his diary as a "log." (Airline pilots and ship captains keep "logs.") The idea of log or diary-keeping might be introduced after watching *The Walton's* on television. John Boy records family events on almost every program. Respect your child's right to privacy by giving him a "safe from siblings" place to keep his log.

As soon as children are able to write they should be encouraged to take notes in the classroom. Notes by their nature are fragmentary.

During study time at home, have the child type or write the notes in sentence form, using the dictionary for spelling and meanings of words. This activity will help to reinforce the information in his memory. It will also make studying for a test much easier.

Teaching a child to type at a young age will help him to make greater gains in spelling, punctuation, capitalization, vocabulary and reading comprehension. Because of the high motivation aspect of typing, the work of the student improves both in quantity and quality.

Television a springboard

Although watching television does not demand participation or response, many educational programs provide outstanding opportunities for family discussion - discussions that will clarify meaning, develop vocabulary, and stimulate interest in learning more about the subject. Many programs can also serve to initiate discussions on values and goals. For example: Many children now reply "paramedic" when asked "What do you want to be when you grow up?" While watching *Emergency* they can visualize a profession that stresses helpfulness and concern for others. After watching this program you could introduce your child to books such as *All About the Human Body* (Random House). The *All About* science series is written at the 4th grade reading level. There are more than fifty books in the series covering a wide range of subjects from rocks to dinosaurs. Even "turned off to reading" children find these books fascinating. Thus, you have used the television program as a springboard for discussion and as encouragement for reading. A wide range of reading is necessary for learning to talk and to write clearly.

Words as tools

Words are the tools with which we understand the thoughts of others. They are also the instruments with which we do our own thinking and with which we express our thoughts to others. A good vocabulary enables us to communicate with precision. If you have ever listened to radio or watched television "man on the street" interviews, you will sense the frustration many of these people feel as they try to communicate.

Speaking, writing, listening to and reading words helps to develop a child's mind. Let's give our children the tools that will enable them to think clearly, make decisions, and deal more effectively with life.

> *"Don't wait for something to turn up.*
> *Get a spade and dig for it."*

Author Unknown

LANGUAGE, A CHILD'S UNFOLDING MIRACLE

Many children suffer the consequences of school failure because remediation for their language deficiencies is not started before they reach school age. All parents do not realize that language, oral and written, is the cornerstone of a child's education. Language is defined as any form of communication used to convey thoughts, ideas, feelings and facts from one individual to another. It is also a mode of internal thought process.

Some specialists believe reading disorders can be attributed to one or more of the following conditions: "(1) Reduced vocabulary; (2) Substandard use of other oral language systems such as phonology (sound features), semantics (meaning), syntax (word order), morphology (tense, person, number, case); (3) Sensory deficits; (4) Perceptual deficits, (5) Memory-retrieval deficits; (6) Poor attention (7) Integrative disorders; (8) Poor instruction; (9) Lack of opportunity." (T.Bangs)

Let us look at the sequential process through which a child develops basic language patterns. You will note that some of these items relate to how the child is reacting to his environment and some of the meaningfulness in his environment. The following milestones, although stated as time, are more in keeping with developmental stages. The time references are only relative.

Three months:

The three-month-old child should have a strong cry and should be able to suck and swallow well. He will react to sudden noises, heed spoken voices and begin to vocalize sounds. He should have a normal voice quality and a meaningful smile. These are beginning moments of language.

Six months:

Several stages of early language development occur at six months. He starts to code some phonemes into possible patterns for later verbal expression. "Identifiable combinations include "ma", "da", "di", "do", (Eisenson) In the babbling stage the child is experimenting with several sound-producing elements of the speech mechanism. His tongue retracts in sucking (this is a basic movement in the production of speech); he laughs aloud, localizes the source of sound (ball, door knocking, etc.) and turns to a speaking voice. Such sounds do not have to be loud to elicit his response.

Nine months:

Little or no drooling at nine months indicates an increased motor control. At this age he waves "bye-bye", understands "no-no," and responds to his name. He will listen to and initiate sound. Although he is creating sounds, he has not yet developed the sensory and motor integration to put these sounds into meaningful words.

One Year:

Between 10 and 18 months, the child usually says his first word. The positive reaction he receives from "mama" and "daddy" encourages him to attempt new words. He will demonstrate his understanding of some words by appropriate behavior. He should be able to point to, or look at, familiar objects or people on request. Continued refinement of his chewing, sucking and swallowing movements is necessary for the production of speech and language.

18 months:

At one and one-half years he has good movement of tongue, lips and palate. "He has a repertoire of words between 3 and 50; some word phrases; and his vocalizations reveal intonational patterns." (Eisenson) He can understand simple questions, identify objects by pointing and can point to his own nose, eye, mouth and hair.

2 years:

At the two-year level he has sufficient vocabulary for naming and for bringing about events. He can follow simple directions without visual clues. He can use nouns, verbs, and some pronouns in simple phrases and sentences. His vocabulary has expanded to approximately 300 words and the majority of the time 25 per cent of his consonant productions are produced proficiently. By this time he is chewing well enough to eat table foods, including meat. He will enjoy being "read to" and shown simple pictures in a book or magazine, and will point out pictures when you ask him to. (Volta Review)

2 ½ years:

The child's vocabulary growth at this age is proportionately greater than at any other period in his life. He speaks with clear communicative intent and uses conventional sentences of three, four and five words. However, his articulation will still include infantilisms. He has good comprehension of speakers in his environment. (Eisenson) At this age he can say or sing short rhymes or songs and enjoys listening to music and to mother singing. He usually reacts to sound by running to look or by telling someone what he hears.

3 years:

By the third year the child begins to identify the usage of things in pictures such as "Show me the one that's good to eat," "Show me the one that you wear," "Show me the one that flies". He can hold up fingers to signify his age, can count to three, repeat five, six or seven-digits (3, 1, 2, etc.), tell how simple objects are used, name objects. He has developed a vocabulary of approximately 500 to 1,000 words, uses several pronouns, adverbs, adjectives and prepositions, and has about 50 to 75 per cent use of all consonants. He will use complete sentences some of the time. Most of his utterances are intelligible to older listeners. (Sturlaugson)

4 years:

At four years he can follow a stage command: "Joe, find Mary and tell her dinner's ready." He should be able to give a connected account of some recent experience. He can give appropriate replics to "What do you do when you're sleepy?" "What do you do when you're hungry?" "What do you do when your cold?" He can count to 5 serially, has a number concept of 2 or 3, identifies two or three colors by name, has a vocabulary of approximately 1,500 words, speaks in complete sentences, and his speech is almost entirely understandable. ((Sturlaugson) "Except for articulation (phonemic production) the linguistic system is essentially that of the adults in his surroundings. He may begin to develop his own "rhetorical" style of favorite words and phrases." (Eisenson)

5 years:

During the fifth year the child now follows a three-stage command, names five colors, counts serially to 10, has number concepts of three and four and has a vocabulary of approximately 2000 words or more. He has the correct usage of all parts of speech and tries to correct his own errors. Although some sounds may be mispronounced, most of the time his language matches the patterns of grammar used by the adults of his family and neighborhood.

By the fifth developmental year (not necessarily chronological year, but development year), a child usually has acquired all the parts of language and speech. Continued development beyond this point is an extension and refinement of the basic language system acquired by the fifth development year.

Caution:

The above outline of language development indicates performances usually achieved at certain development age levels. Because of individual differences among wide varieties of populations, it is not the EXACT age at which a child demonstrates the learning of certain things, but the ORDER in which he learns related items, that is of primary importance. Remember, you are his model.

"He who helps a child helps humanity with immediateness which no other help given to human creature in any other stage of human life can possibly give again."

Phillip Brooks

IS YOUR CHILD READY FOR KINDERGARTEN

Soon your child will be starting his first year in school; Kindergarten is an important time for a child because it is his introduction to an experience that may help to form his goals, aspiration, trade and occupation. Failure in kindergarten may set the pattern for subsequent failure in his total school experience.

The supposition that at a given age level all children are ready for certain tasks is not supported by medical, psychological or academic proof. Each child in your household has grown at his own rate in various areas. The child you are now thinking of enrolling in kindergarten has grown at his own rate. Attending school does help a child to develop, but he must have certain skills before the approaches to development can be made.

The skills needed by the child for kindergarten are developmental ones, both mental and physical. It is our hope that we offer some guidelines to help you determine whether your child is ready for kindergarten. The maturity of your child is not to be confused with "how smart he is." Only a small percentage of children are unable to attend a regular class because of some intellectual deficiency. However, research has shown us that a much larger percentage are not ready due to normal development in a physiological way.

Most children who are not ready for kindergarten, but are placed there because of age, experience feelings of failure and dissatisfaction which are not overcome in school at a later date. Kindergarten programs are becoming more sophisticated as our children are exposed to reading readiness and arithmetic readiness programs and other areas of the curriculum. If there is too wide a gap between what is expected of them and what they really can do, failure becomes incorporated into their self concept. It is healthy for a child to learn how to fail, but only if his self concept is strong enough to handle it.

Sometimes, if a child is withheld for a very short time, it gives him a chance to mature. At this age children grow rapidly in the perceptual and motor ability needed to do school work.

The following checklists may be a helpful guide for you to determine how ready your child is for kindergarten. Go over the checklist now. If these guidelines suggest that your child is not ready, you still have nine months left in which to prepare him for the experience. Recheck your child the latter part of August. In this way you can determine his growth.

READINESS CHECKLIST

Growth and Age

1. Will your child be 5 years old on or before Dec. 1?
2. Is your child at or better than the following norms in weight and height? Boys: weight, 40 lbs; height, 43 inches.
    Girls: weight, 37 lbs; height, 42 inches.
3. Can strangers easily understand your child's speech?

General Activity Related to Growth: Can your child:

4. Pay attention to short stories and read and answer simple questions about them?
5. Draw and color beyond scribbles?
6. Tie a knot?
7. Zip or button up a coat?
8. Walk backward for a distance of 5 to 6 feet?
9. Stand on one foot for 5 to 10 seconds?
10. Alternate feet walking downstairs?
11. Walk a straight line?

12. Fasten buttons he can see?
13. Tell left hand from right hand?
14. Use knife for spreading jam or butter?
15. Take care of toilet needs by himself?
16. Travel alone in neighborhood to friend's house?
17. Be away from home (and you) 2-3 hours without being upset?
18. Cross a residential street safely?

REMEMBERING: Can your child:

19. Repeat a series of 4 numbers without practice,
    such as "say after me 6-1-7-4"?
20. Repeat 8-10 word sentences if you say them once?
    "The boy ran all the way home from the store."
21. Remember instructions and carry out 2 or 3 simple errands or
    tasks in the home after being told once? ("Pick up the book, bring
    me the pencil, and close the door.")

UNDERSTANDING: Can your child:

22. Tell you the meaning of simple words like bicycle, apple,
    shoe, hammer, water, shirt, horse?
23. Count 4 objects?
24. Supply the last word to all the following statements?
    Mother is a woman; father is a _____
    A fire is hot; an ice cube is _____
    A plane goes fast; a turtle goes_____
25. Put together a simple puzzle of 3-6 pieces?
26. Tell what parts are missing if you draw a stick picture of a
    person and leave off an arm or leg?
27. Draw or copy a circle, triangle and square?
28. Name correctly these drawings?

GENERAL KNOWLEDGE: Can your child tell you:

29. How many feet he has?
30. How many ears he has?
31. Which goes faster, a motor scooter or bike?
32. What or where meat comes from?
33. What things are made of, like cars, shoes, etc.
34. What a key is for?
35. What eyes are for?
36. What his ears are used for?
37. The names of 3 or 4 colors that you point out?
38. Tell in what way a sweater, shoe and hat are the same?

ATTITUDES AND INTERESTS:

39. Do you have books, magazines and newspapers in your home that your child looks at?
40. Is your child unafraid of going to school?
41. Does your child ask often of going to school?
42. Does your child pretend to read?
43. Have you attempted to create in your child the idea of looking forward to school experiences rather than the fear of school?

USING THE RESULTS

Count the number of items you were able to answer with a "yes" response. This number, the approximate state of readiness for school and possible action to be taken follow:

40 to 43 – readiness reasonably assured – school entrance

35 to 39 – readiness very probable – school entrance

31 to 34 – readiness questionable – consultation with school principal recommended

26 to 30 – readiness doubtful – consultation with school principal recommended

25 or below – readiness unlikely – consultation with school principal recommended.

Each item on this scale must be considered to have individual variations for all children, depending on growth and experience. The total score can only be used as a rough index to readiness and not as an absolute determination of school readiness.

A question often asked by parents is: "When will my child be ready to read?" One answer to this important question might be that a child is ready for reading instruction when his physiological development and the cumulative effect of all his experiences enable him to learn the response that the school wishes to teach.

Another way to define readiness for reading is to draw up a list of the skills, knowledge, and other qualities that a child needs when learning to read. The following list has been selected from the Harper and Row Basic Reading Program checklist "Earmarks of Readiness."

PHYSICAL: Good health – results of a physical examination are favorable; good vision – both at near point and far point; good hearing – adequate acuity; hears what is said in the classroom; adequate motor-control – good coordination in tracing, cutting, and handling instructional materials.

SOCIAL AND EMOTIONAL: Sharing – allows others to use materials in his possession; listening – permits others to speak without constant interruptions; obeying – accepts direction by teacher readily and without resentment; courtesy – awaits his turn in games and in using classroom equipment; respecting others – accepts decision of a group; respecting property – takes care of equipment and materials, cleans up own mess without being told.

INTELLECTUAL: Attention – can pay attention to a task for at least 15 minutes; communication – pronounces words correctly, uses complete sentences, speaks with good voice, articulation and rhythm; understanding – know meaning of appropriate terms, has rudimentary knowledge of numbers, can identify selected colors; memory – can memorize birth date and home address, repeat a simple sentence without error, follow a series of three directions in correct order; relationships

– recognizes common elements among unlike things, understands relationships of opposites, able to classify objects such as items found in the kitchen, in a grocery, or things Father likes.

HUMOR - LIFE'S OIL

Humor is like oil in the machinery of life. It can release tension, be more effective than nagging, help to develop abstract thinking ability in children and make life more fun.

Humor is based on such variables as an exaggeration of a known situation, a play on words or the surprise element. Thus, to appreciate the humor in a situation, a child must understand his environment.

Pleasure from humor comes from the child's certainty that the situation does not really exist. The joke or situation is not funny to the child who identifies too closely with it. Stupidity, clumsy, or aggressive themes may be too suggestive of errors the child makes in his everyday life. These themes are best omitted until the child has a good self concept.

Adjusting for the child's age and level of development one could start with comic strips, jokes from Boy's Life magazine, or selected sections from the Reader's Digest such as: Life in These United States; Laughter The Best Medicine; Toward More Picturesque Speech; All in A Day's Work; Quotable Quotes; or the jokes at the end of each article. Ask the child "Could this really happen?" or "Why is this funny?" As the child explains he is getting practice in verbal expression that will later help him to organize his thoughts, write a clear composition and answer essay questions at school. This activity also provides an opportunity to guide his vocabulary, sentence structure and pronunciation. When you explain to the child why the situation is humorous you are teaching him to think on an abstract level. Abstract thinking is an important dimension of general intelligence.

To understand the humor in cartoons and comic strips it is often necessary to observe small details. Observing details is essential for accurate reading.

Comic strips have special codes and symbols that help one to appreciate the humor. Exclamation points or question marks above a character's head that represent surprise or curiosity; horizontal lines suggest speed of movement; light bulbs illustrate understanding or a new idea, etc. Many children need to have these symbols explained before the cartoon has meaning for them. Explaining these codes provides a lead-in opportunity to discuss the use and function of punctuation marks.

SOCIAL AWARENESS

Comic strips can help to reach social awareness. When one cuts each individual square unit, shuffles them and asks the child to place them in the proper order, the child may understand that certain behavior logically follows other behavior. Children who lack social skills often do not understand this.

It is so easy to minimize tension in the home with humor. For example, a mother who felt the children's noise level had exceeded the sound barrier said with a smile and a twinkle in her eye, "Let's keep the noise down to a steady roar." The children laughed and lowered their voices. After a parental request one child said, "Mother, if I didn't know you better, I would almost think you were nagging." Mom replied, "Oops, you caught me!" They both laughed. But the significant thing was that the requests were honored without tension.

A child with a sense of humor and a good self concept can laugh at his own foibles. Seeing the humorous side of an adverse situation demonstrates his flexibility to adjust. He will also have many friends because others will enjoy being around him.

"You can get friction for nothing, but harmony costs courtesy and self control."

Elbert Hubbard

GROWING YOUNGSTERS NEED ENCOURAGEMENT

Children thrive on encouragement. In the book, *Encouraging Children to Learn*, Dinkmeyer and Dreikurs state: "Encouragement is so crucial that the effect of any action is actually determined by the extent to which the child is or is not encouraged." Although this book was written to help school teachers understand the encouragement process, we must remember that parents are teachers. A child spends more time in his home environment than he spends with his teacher. Thus, parents have tremendous opportunities to encourage their children by believing in them.

The result of any encouraging act depends upon how the child perceives and responds to it. Usually we perceive only what we want or expect to see. This "biased apperception" is highly dependent upon one's self-image. Our need, then, is to understand each child's interpretation of his environmental experiences.

Man creates his own experiences to be consistent with his "biased apperception". Consequently, one's environment is less important than the attitude one takes toward his environment. When we recognize the extraordinary power individuals have in determining their own actions, in setting their own goals, and in bringing about their expectations we realize the significance of encouragement. "Whoever alters a person's expectations changes his behavior." (Dreikurs)

We all desire to belong to someone or something. The need to find one's significance through "belonging" explains many kinds of behavior. Since belonging requires cooperation in social relationships, one of the most important things a child can learn at home is social responsibility – caring for what happens to others. Numerous studies have revealed that more individuals lose jobs because of an inability to get along with others than because of inability to do the work assigned.

Gordon Allport said, "Goal striving is the essence of personality." Studied closely, a child's actions reveal his goals. His private logic will determine how he uses his abilities. It follows that a frame of reference for an encouragement plan can be obtained through observation of behavior:

1. Try to view situations through the eyes of the child.
2. Watch for purposes and goals in his actions.
3. Record behavior and look for recurring patterns.
4. Be aware of his age and level of development.

As outlined by Dreikurs, the person who encourages:

1. Places value on the child as he is.
2. Shows a faith in the child that enables the child to have faith in himself.
3. Has faith in the child's ability; wins the child's confidence while building his self-respect.
4. Recognizes a job "well done". Gives recognition for effort.
5. Utilizes the group to facilitate and enhance the development of the child.
6. Integrates the family group so that the child can be sure of his place in it.
7. Assists in the development of skills sequentially and psychologically paced to permit success.
8. Recognizes and focuses on strengths and assets.
9. Utilizes the interests of the child to energize instruction.

Every child has potentialities that can be developed when one focuses on his assets and believes he is worth the effort involved in helping him. Children whose learning is not impeded by pressure, by rebellion, or by a sense of failure achieve significantly more. They are spontaneous, eager to learn and cooperative.

On the other hand, a discouraged child lacks confidence and assumes that he has no chance. He has hoped against hope, tried without expectation of success, and has finally given up. Discouraged children often solidify this failure at an early age and become successful failures.

Loneliness is the basic psychology course of a failure identity. Lonely in this case means sociologically and culturally deprived. "Disadvantaged" is riding high in the saddle right now, but both words indicate the child has not had an equal opportunity to make contact with responsible people. Most discouraged children do not have many friends. Helping them to become involved in cooperative relationships will be the first step toward helping them over the wall to the success side. The true method of motivation is involvement.

Parents can help their children to make plans and establish goals. The goals and plans for their realization should be developed by the child. He should be guided to make short-term goals that are successive approximations toward his long-term goal. Small commitments permit success experiences that encourage. For example:

Educational goals

1. Establish a specific long-term goal. (General statement of "I want good grades" is not enough.)

2. List short-term goals that are successive approximations toward the long-term goals.

3. Determine and write down what you will give in exchange for the goals.

4. Specify a definite time when each short-term goal will be realized.

5. Outline a plan for achieving these goals and start now.

6. Read the written statement aloud twice daily – the last thing before you go to bed at night and the first thing in the morning.

7. Make visual pictures of your goals as having already been achieved. (By programming your brain with visual pictures of success, the subconscious will actively work toward achieving these goals.)

Encouragement is a day by day, moment by moment process. Suggested in this view is the belief that an environment able to respond to the child's needs constructively could result in a higher level of functioning.

"Once, someone said something nice about me, and, all undeserved though I knew it to be, I treasured it there on my heart's deepest shelf till one day I quite surprised even myself by honestly making an effort to be that nice thing that somebody said about me!"

Helen Marshall

PREPARATION IMPORTANT IN DEVELOPING READING SKILLS

One of the great advances in fighting disease was the development of preventive medicine. With a premium on preparation, evidence mounts that we can also prevent many learning difficulties even before the child knows he has a problem.

A study in Denver revealed these generalizations about first grade children who were having difficulty with reading:

1. The children couldn't organize their thoughts in logical sequence.
2. They couldn't verbalize picture content.
3. Their left-to-right orientation was non-existent.
4. Their ability to hear sounds was weak.
5. The children lacked ability to identify letters.
6. They experienced many reversals, vertical and horizontal, in seeing and writing letters.
7. They had poor motor coordination.
8. Their attention span was short.
9. Many of the children had social adjustment problems.

Since children do not grow at the same rate, parents must be ready to offer their child the developmental experiences he needs in preparation for success. Many children have failed in reading because they were not ready to begin to read. Therefore, it is important to determine a child's level of successful performance in the developmental skills so that he can begin when he can succeed.

Sequencing

Activities which require the child to consider logical order:

- Encourage the child to tell daily happenings in correct order: "What did we do first?" etc.

- Have the child help with household tasks that require sequence and have him verbalize the sequence after the task is completed.

- Dramatize the sequence of the child's day through action games and songs, i.e., use the "Mulberry Bush" tune and sing: "This is the way we dress ourselves.", "This is the way we wash our hands.", etc.

- Provide opportunities for the child to put pictures in a logical sequence. Read selected newspaper "funnies" to the child. Cut out each square unit and ask the child to arrange them in order.

- Ask the child to tell a familiar story with leading questions: How did the story begin? What happened next? Then what happened? How did the story end?

A scale for evaluating a child's language ability in interpreting pictures is from *Necessary Pre-School Experiences for Comprehending Reading* by Marion Monroe:

- Select pictures in which two or more characters are involved in an interesting activity.

- Ask the child "What is this picture about?"

Record the child's verbal response and determine the level of the step on which he responds:

Step 1. The child shrugs and doesn't respond verbally to the question. He may name objects in the picture, i.e. "dog", "boy", etc.

Step 2. The child describes action, i.e., "The dog is jumping up.", "The baby is eating."

Step 3. The child verbalizes a relationship between characters or objects, i.e. "The boy's playing ball with the dog."

Step 4. The child gives relationships of time, place, cause, and effect, i.e., "The boys are building a bird house. They will put it in a tree so a bird can build a nest in it."

Step 5. The child perceives and responds to feelings and emotional reactions of the characters and draws a conclusion, i.e., "It's a dark night and the children are scared. They're singing songs around the fire. Wild animals won't come near the fire." Children who have not reached Step

3 or Step 4 on this scale probably lack sufficient language ability to interpret a picture in a primer and respond to the text. They need many experiences which will develop verbal skills.

A rough assessment of language ability may be secured from these items: Ask the child to say "yes" if the statement is true, "no" if not true. – Roses walk; dogs bark; houses run; cows give milk; houses are to live in; and chairs are to hear.

Understanding verbal directions: "Touch the table and your shoes," etc.

Auditory association of ideas: "Name all the animals you can." "How are a pig and a cow alike?"

Visual association of ideas: Classify pictures into categories such as farm animals, machinery, plants, etc. Child is shown two pictures and asked how they are alike and how different, i.e., car and truck; table and chair, etc.

Problem solving: "If you couldn't find your sweater, how would you go about finding it?"

Ask the child to repeat several simple sentences. Does he omit or add words? Does he change the order of the words in the sentence? The following activities to help develop a meaningful vocabulary are from *How to Increase Reading Ability,* by Albert J. Harris.

- Use pictures for introducing new concepts.

- Acting games develop meaning for words. Children can act out nouns (animals, etc.), verbs (walk, jump, run, hop), adverbs (quickly, quietly), and prepositions (under, behind, in).

- Visits to school, stores, fire station, etc., enable a child to develop new concepts and vocabulary through experience and discussion.

- Puppets and simple costumes provide avenues through which the child may lose his self-consciousness. (Visit a rummage sale just before closing time to get interesting items for costumes.)

- Activities such as telephone conversations, radio broadcasts, and dramatizations provide opportunities for growth in language ability.

- Encourage the growth of vocabulary through questions about familiar objects and pictures.

- Help the child to develop a descriptive vocabulary through the visual experience of comparing and examining details: large – small; round – square; to the left – to the right; above – below.

Left – right orientation

There is considerable overlap between the area of left-right orientation, body concept, and spatial orientation. The initial awareness of the two sides of the body and their differences later becomes the basis for concepts of direction in space. "If there is no left and right inside the organism the directional characteristics of b and d disappear." (Kephart)

- Give the child a play watch or loose rubber band to put on his left wrist. Say to the child, "Point to your nose. It is in the middle of your face. Everything on the left side of your nose is on the left side." Do the same with the right side. Say, "Point to your right eye, your left ear, etc."

- Games help develop right and left concepts, i.e., Simon says: "Touch your right foot, touch your left ear and put your left hand on your right ear."

- Have the child fetch things in the house. Ask him to bring you an item from the left-hand side of the closet, etc.

- Trace child's hand on paper and draw in fingernails. Say, "This is your right hand." Do the same with left hand. Ask, "Are these pictures of the back or the palms of your hands?" Give the child a simple sequence to follow in matching: left hand, right hand, left hand, etc.

- Make up a large card with several rows of pictures (newspaper "funnies" or rows of small pictures.) Ask the child to name the pictures noting the order he uses.

- Place ten blocks in a row. Ask the child to count them, noting whether he goes from left to right or from right to left.

- When reading to your child place your finger under the words as you read. Draw his attention to the fact that you start reading at the left side of the page and progress to the right.

Body Image

- Have the child lie on the floor on a large sheet of paper. Trace his body outline with a thick crayon. Ask your child to fill in the details with a crayon.

- Ask your child to draw the very best person he can. Note incorrect concepts such as arms and legs attached to head, etc.

- Take a picture of a child from a catalog or magazine. Cut the body in half lengthwise and paste it on cardboard or another sheet of paper. The child can use the existing half as a guide while he completes the picture. This same idea can be used with other items to help develop an awareness of spatial relationships.

- Make a picture of a person and cut it into several parts. The child reassembles the parts to make the whole.

- Give your child a green block and a red block and ask him to follow directions: put the green block in front of the red block; put the red block on top of the green block; put the green block behind the red block; put the red block beside the green block; put the green block under the red block.

- Use three small toy cars: red, blue, green: pick up the blue car in your left hand; pick up the red car in your right hand; move the green car forward; move the red car backward; lift the green car over the red car and put it in front of the red car.

- Use directions involving the relationship of the body to other objects: stand in the circle; step out of the circle; stand in the box; jump over a block; climb on a chair; go around a table; crawl under a table.

- Use two pegboards (or celotex acoustical square tiles with about 12 holes across and 12 holes down and golf tees.) Make a simple design on one board and ask the child to duplicate the design on his board. Always begin with a simple design which he can make successfully. Note any tendency to turn or reverse the pattern.

TESTS TO HELP CHILDREN PREPARE FOR READING

Many children have failed in reading because they were not ready to begin to read. Evidence continues to mount that preparation can prevent many learning difficulties. Let's review the generalizations about first grade children who were having difficulty with reading:

1. The children couldn't organize their thoughts in logical sequence.
2. They couldn't verbalize picture content.
3. Their left-to-right orientation was non-existent.
4. Their ability to hear sounds was weak.
5. The children lacked ability to identify letters.
6. They experienced many reversals, vertical and horizontal, in seeing and writing letters.
7. They had poor motor coordination.
8. Their attention span was short.
9. Many of the children had social adjustment problems.

Auditory discrimination

"Poor auditory discrimination is prevalent among poor readers. Unless a child can hear the difference between two spoken words he cannot learn to associate each of them consistently with the printed symbol. This skill can be improved by listening." (Albert J. Harris, "Effective Reading")

Say pairs of words to the child. Tell the child to say "yes" if the words are the same and say "no" if the words are different. (Some children may need to have the meanings of the words "same" and "different" explained to them.) Jam – jack, lip – log, pin – pen, jump – jug, let – ladder, red – rest, big – big, him – hen, Micky – Nicky, eat – catch, his – his, and pan – pan.

Patricia Nordberg

These listening activities may be helpful for a child who has difficulty hearing similarities and differences:

- Without looking ask the child to identify the sound he hears when someone sharpens a pencil, knocks on the door, drops a shoe, closes the window.

- Have child close his eyes and try to identify outside noises.

- Read jingles and rhymes and ask the child to listen for rhyming words.

- Initiate games such as: "I went to the store, I bought bananas." Encourage the child to add a word beginning with the same sound, i.e., ball, balloon, beans, etc.

Ask child to listen for rhyming words in couplets: Here is Bill, he lives on a hill, etc.

- Have child finish rhymes by adding the last word: My name is Sue, my eyes are _____.

Observable behaviors

- Inattention and lack of interest in conversation around him, or unusual concentrated attention on the individual speaking.

- Failure to answer questions or failure to answer correctly.

- Repeatedly asking, "What did you say?"

- Tilting of the head to one side to bring best ear nearer to the speaker.

- Flat, nasal, or monotonous voice.

- Bewildered expression when directions are given.

- Fatigue from the constant effort to hear.

- Incorrect pronunciation of familiar words.

Auditory memory differentiates good readers from poor readers. These activities may prove helpful for children who lack auditory memory.

- Rote teaching of songs and poems motivates and strengthens auditory memory.

- Following directions successfully demands listening and remembering; i.e., send the child on an errand which requires that he remember more than one thing. Make it a practice not to ask him to remember too many things at the beginning of his auditory memory training. It is important that he does not need to ask that directions be repeated.

- Memory games such as: "I went to a farm. I saw a horse, a pig, a sheep, and a goat. Now tell me the names of the animals I saw."

- It is helpful to combine auditory memory and association. Present a series of words that have a relationship such as cow, horse, pig, goat. Ask the child to repeat the series of words in correct sequence and to describe the relationship.

- Listening to stories provides a need to remember. Ask the child to retell the story in sequence.

- Tell a story, and then retell it leaving something out. Ask the child what was left out.

- Have child memorize his telephone number and street address.

- Memorize "Old MacDonald Had a Farm", and similar songs.

Visual perception

"A child who has a lag in his perceptual development may have such difficulty in recognizing objects and their relationship to each other in space that it causes him to perceive the world in a distorted fashion. The confusion with which he perceives visual symbols makes academic learning difficult no matter how intelligent he is." (Frostig)

Eye-hand coordination, the ability to sense spatial relationships and the ability to focus on one stimulus in the midst of many stimuli are some of the important aspects of visual perception.

Ask the child to draw geometric forms:

- Show a picture of a circle. Say "Draw one that looks like this." Do the same for a square and a triangle. The manner is which the forms are produced is more important than the production. Note tremors, rotation of designs, and segmenting of forms. Observe whether or not the child completes the form as a whole, or one line at a time.

- Provide a shoe string with a knot in one end. Ask the child to string six large primary beads or large straight macaroni.

- Ask the child to draw a straight line between two dots.

- Show these letters: V, P, D, E, M, L. Ask the child to copy the letters.

- Cutting helps develop the child's ability to coordinate eyes and hands more effectively. Have the child cut on heavy black lines. Use light cardboard or construction paper to avoid easy tearing.

- Cut geometric figures outlined with heavy straight lines such a square, rectangle, triangle.

- Cut on heavy curved lines and circles. Cut very simple pictures outlined with a heavy line.

- Cut fringe on place mats, cut Chinese lanterns. Fold, cut and make "surprise" cuttings.

- Use blunt scissors to cut modeling clay that has been rolled.

- Use manipulative toys; peg boards, form boards, jigsaw puzzles. (Save front and back panels from cereal and crackers boxes. On unprinted side draw heavy lines for cutting. After cutting, the child turns the cardboard over and reassembles.)

- Provide handwork materials: Paste, paint, crayons, modeling clay, wood pieces.

To coordinate sensory channels and to develop small muscle control, allow child to touch articles such as sandpaper, cotton, a stone, a smooth mirror, a piece of velvet, etc. After each one ask: "What else is hard? What else is smooth?" etc.

_ Let the child play with plastic bottles with screw tops and nuts and bolts.

- Permit child to place key in lock and turn door knob when entering house.

- Turning pages of a book.

- Folding paper vertically, horizontally, diagonally.

- Baton twirling (Dowling or shortened broom handles can be used.)

- Connecting dots to make a picture. Teach him how to write the letters in his name by connecting dots. Make the first letter in upper case and the following letters in his name in lower case. (When children come to school knowing how to write their name in capital letters the teacher has to re-teach them.)

Figure-ground

Children who are disturbed by varied stimuli in background material need practice in fixing their attention on one stimulus. This activity must begin simply and gradually develop in complexity.

- Superimpose the outline of a house upon the outline of a tree. Ask the child to outline the tree with a crayon.

- Superimpose the outline of a triangle upon the outline of a square. Ask the child to outline the triangle with a crayon.

- Draw the outline of several geometric figures superimposed upon each other. Ask the child to outline each figure in a different color.

- Look at a picture. Ask the child to find the largest boy, the tallest tree, the green apple on the tree, etc.

- Can the child find designated objects within varied background materials? Find all the red things in the room. Find all the living things in the room, etc.

"One of the specific and most clearly reading-related aspects of development in pre-reading instruction is that of visual discrimination. This includes the ability to notice slight differences in form, line, size, etc., and to recognize when things look just alike." (Dr. Dorothy Koehring, "Getting Ready to Read")

- Cut many geometric forms in many colors. Ask the child to sort all the red triangles, blue triangles, red circles, blue circles, etc.

- Provide a large card with many geometric forms drawn on it. Matching forms are drawn on individual cards (circle, square, triangle, diamond and rectangle). Have the child match one card at a time to the large card.

- Ask the child to match 2 inch letters on a large card. Make individual letters 2 inches tall on individual cards. Hold up one card and say "Find one that looks like this one."

Visual Concerns:
- Seeing objects double.
- Headaches, dizziness or nausea associated with the use of eyes.
- Body rigidity while looking at distant objects.
- Undue sensitivity to light.

- Crossed eyes – turning in or out.
- Red-rimmed, crusted or swollen lids.
- Frequent sties.
- Watering or bloodshot eyes.
- Burning or itching of eyes or eyelids.
- Tilting head to one side.
- Tending to rub eyes.
- Closing or covering one eye.

Visual memory

Visual memory is the ability to remember stimuli presented visually. These activities may provide for the motivation and reinforcement of visual memory:

- Show three objects. Cover one and ask "Which one did I hide?" Do the same with four and then five objects, etc.
- Show the child a picture. Remove it and ask him to tell everything he remembers about the picture.
- The child looks at a page in a picture dictionary or catalog and tries to remember as many pictures as he can.
- Show a circle, square, triangle, one at a time. Allow the child 5 seconds to look at it. Remove the geometric form and ask the child to draw it from memory.
- The child observes three or four objects on a table in a certain order. The objects are rearranged while the child's eyes are closed and he replaces them in the original order. (Gradually add more objects.)
- Make a bead chain design. Remove one object and ask the child which one is missing.

The ideas suggested above are not meant to be an exhaustive list. Rather, they are intended to stimulate the parent to think of creative ideas adaptive to the individual home situation.

"You will find as you look back upon your life that the moments that stand out above everything else are the moments when you have done things in a spirit of love."

Henry Drummond

THE DEVELOPMENTAL STAGES OF LEARNING

Educational literature recognizes six general stages of learning. In sequential order they are: gross-motor stage; motor-perceptual stage; perceptual-motor stage; perceptual stage; perceptual-conceptual stage; and conceptual stage. Although there is some overlapping, the stages are hierarchical, building upon themselves in a related series.

To avoid being confused by semantics, remember that perceptual processes are brain operations that involve interpreting and organizing the physical elements of the stimulus. Cognition involves thinking, meaningful language, or problem-solving processes.

In his book *Success Through Play,* Kephart states, "There is evidence that the efficiency of the higher thought processes can be no better than the basic motor abilities upon which they are based." Walking, running, skipping, hopping, throwing, catching, jumping are neuromuscular activities that require balance, strength, endurance, timing and coordination. A child rarely develops these skills while sitting passively in front of a television set.

Studies of kindergarten children judged to be immature by their teachers revealed these consistent observations: immature motor performance, inadequate language skills and insufficient attention span. Many children who are later identified as "learning disabled" were considered immature when they were 5 years old.

Maturation unfolds with stimulation

Perhaps an ideal combination of parents for a child would be a loving mother with degrees in speech therapy, special education and school psychology, and a father of the Albert Schweitzer type. In lieu of this unlikely combination, similar progress can be achieved by parents interested in seeking information on how to help their children. For instance, there are many facets of everyday familial interaction that can be channeled into learning experiences. It is hoped that using every opportunity to teach will become a way of life for the family. The suggestions offered may be used as cues for habilitation. Each family will want to expand and develop flexible adaptations suitable to the individual child. When working with your child remember the advice of the skilled golfer: "Keep your eye on the ball, follow through, but don't press."

Children learn best through activity. Doing, touching, handling, brings an element of discovery. Activity also stimulates the brain to help facilitate the learning process.

The kitchen and father's workshop are ideal places to refine motor coordination. Think of the variety of finger movements in slicing, dicing, chopping, paring, peeling, stirring, grating, pouring, etc. If pouring presents a problem, let the child practice pouring solid materials from one container to another. Language develops as the child is taught the word that describes each action. Descriptive words such as sticky, hot, lukewarm, cool, greasy are felt and experienced. An awareness of sequence, order and system develops as a child helps with dinner preparations.

For example, the learning experiences from preparing a package of jello are multiple: The child measure and pours water into a pan; he adds the jello powder when the water boils; he stirs the jello until it dissolves; perhaps with assistance he pours the liquid into another container; he peeks into the refrigerator and observes the jello changing from a liquid into a solid; he serves it at dinner with a sense of accomplishment. Mother has invested time but the dividends were great.

The rewards are equally as great when father slows his tempo to work side by side with his child in the workshop or yard. Motor skills are developed when a child is taught how to pound a nail into a board, is permitted to create something from wood or other scraps, and later to paint or stain the new creation. To protect the child, his clothing, and the general environment when he is staining, supply: grocery sacks to put under the item; one of father's old shirts buttoned down the back; clear plastic bags over the hands secured at the wrists with rubber bands; two small squares of cloth from discarded undershirts (one for applying the stain and one for wiping the excess). To the above add patience and sense of humor.

A close relationship develops between parent and child when these "helping" periods are salted with encouragement for effort and reinforcement for improvement.

A Harvard early education specialist who spent 17 years researching the development of children from birth to age 6 concluded that "A well-developed child of 3 has the same special abilities as a well-developed 6 year old. The difference is only a matter of refinement." Burton White maintained that what parents do, or don't do, in the early developmental years can make a lifetime of difference for the child.

"The rung of a ladder was never meant to rest upon, but only to hold a man's foot long enough to enable him to put the other somewhat higher."

Thomas Huxley

SELF ESTEEM IMPORTANT TO THE GROWING CHILD

During early childhood one psychological characteristic, perhaps more than any other, helps a child grow emotionally and feel self-sufficient. Self-esteem gives a child a sense of worth for his own sake – for his own capabilities, and for himself as a human being with unique qualities. It is woven into a child's personality from threads of constructive experiences and the warm approval of others. Every child needs someone who can say, "I wonder what sort of human experience this child needs with me? And how can I best give it?"

Dorothy Briggs' book, *Your Child's Self-Esteem,* offers parents a blueprint with step by step specifics. Each child, though individually unique, has the same psychological needs: to love and be loved, and to feel worthwhile to himself and to others. This book helps you to see all growth and behavior against the backdrop of the child's search for identity and self-respect.

"High self-esteem is not conceit; it is your child's quiet comfort about being who he is." (Briggs). Your child's self-image forms the core of his personality and can limit or expand his individual accomplishment. Briggs feels that helping children build high self-esteem is the key to successful parenthood.

Psychological mirror

A parent is the psychological mirror a child uses to build his identity. Brothers, sisters, teachers, and all significant others in his life are additional mirrors. A child not only takes in others' descriptions of himself, he also absorbs their attitudes towards those qualities. Attitudes toward a child's abilities are more important than the possession of them. "The key to the kind of identity your child builds is directly tied to how he's been judged. What goes on between your youngster and those around him, consequently, is of central importance." (Briggs) When a child receives many positive messages from his family he is better able to withstand negative messages coming from outside relationships. Positive reflections are the sunshine in life.

One of the outstanding chapters in *Your Child's Self-Esteem* is titled "Polishing Parental Mirrors". Briggs felt that occasionally looking at a child's world from his point of view helps one to make allowances for what to expect. She suggests that since parental expectations affect the quality of their "mirroring", they should examine them from time to time. If introspection unearths some of the circumstances that affect parental behavior, perhaps the parent can deal with it rather than to react blindly with expectations that meet his needs alone. She further recommended that the parent write each expectation down and look at it in the light of the following questions:

Why do I have this expectation? Where did it come from? What's in it for me? Is it based on my needs or my child's? What purpose does it serve? Does it realistically fit this particular child at his age and with his temperament and background?

She commented that although an honest inventory may be painful, it is usually a forerunner to change. Frederick Perls said, "You do unto others what you do unto yourself." Self acceptance enables you to accept others.

Many parents who care deeply have children who feel unloved. "Love is not necessarily communicated by physical affection, constantly setting aside your own needs, over-protection, high expectation, time and gifts." (Briggs) It is valuing your child just because he exists. Parents will eventually resent being their child's personal servant – martyrdom is not love. Over-protection undermines self-confidence. Sometimes our need to be needed prevents the child's need, which is not to need us, from being fulfilled. *From the moment of birth, a parent's task is to train the child to become independent of him.* Independence is the cornerstone of self-confidence. Observe a child's joy when he can dress himself, catch a ball, ride a bike, etc. Each achievement gives him confidence to reach out for a new experience. Numerous studies have indicated that a child tries to live up to parental expectations. Yet, if these expectations are so unrealistic as to be developmentally impossible for the child, he begins to feel inadequate and unloved. Children need to feel loved apart from their achievements. Temporarily setting aside your own world to be with your child is a constructive beginning in developing high self-esteem for your child. Genuine encounter is focused attention with an "all-hereness" quality. The amount of time is less important than the quality of your focused attention. Indifference is the opposite of love. Direct involvement nourishes self-worth because it says "I care".

Hurts inevitable

Hurts are inevitable while living in the psychologically close quarters of the family unit. The bruises heal quickly, however, on a child who has a positive self-image and a sense of humor. High self-esteem frees him so that he can laugh at his own foibles. Teach him, by example, how to observe the humorous side of everyday living situations. Humor is oil in the machinery of life. A child with a sense of humor has more opportunities for positive feedback because others enjoy being around him.

Briggs devotes individual chapters to the six ingredients of psychological safety: Trust, Nonjudgment, Being Cherished, "Owning" Feeling, Empathy and Unique Growing.

She feels that trust is the anchor in a psychologically safe environment. Children can trust when those around him are open about their feelings. The repression of true feelings is rarely totally effective. Since only seven per cent of communication is done verbally, feelings of which we are unaware are communicated directly or indirectly to others. Genuine honesty is sensed by children and interpreted as dependability. When the parent's attitudes and feelings are clear to him, his communication to the child loses its ambiguity. When his feelings are hidden or disguised the total message to the child is contradictory and inspires distrust. The foundation of a supportive relationship is confidence in the supportive figure. Trust communicates security.

Many children receive focused attention only when they misbehave. Then they get it fast! Attention only during misbehavior reinforces the misdeed and increases the possibility that it will reoccur. Misbehavior is often a cry for love, acceptance, and the nourishment that comes from positive social interaction with others. Even though they need reactions to set limits on their behavior, they can be spared from labels. Labels become incorporated into a child's self-image and he will learn to behave consistent with the labeling. In general, "You" followed by a noun or adjective is a judgment. An "I" reaction tells the child how you feel and should be specific to the situation. Briggs cites examples:

"You-reactions"

> "You're such a slowpoke!"
> "You're messy!"
> "You're a liar."
> "You're lazy."
> "You have good taste."

Children like who they are when they feel "special". Cherishing is finding him dear in spite of intermittent irritations. A child is a miracle that we live with every day – A miracle we often take for granted. If we treated our friends as we sometimes treat our children, how many friends would we have? Few of us would put-down, humiliate, embarrass or bark orders to our friends. The Golden Rule should also be applied in our relationships with our children.

Praise important

Sometimes our children don't feel cherished because we focus on what's wrong rather than what's right. If Joey brought his spelling test home with 3 errors, but with 17 words spelled correctly, how often would we hear: "How wonderful that you spelled 17 words correctly. Perhaps you can tell me what clues you used to help you remember them." Then later: "Let's see if together we can figure out some remembering clues on these other three." If you suggest in such a way that the remembering clues are his own idea, you will have given him an opportunity for creativity. Additionally, you have taught him how to study for the next spelling test.

You respect your child's uniqueness when you avoid asking him to match his feelings and reactions to yours. We are talking about the freedom to feel, not the freedom to act. Each individual has a different psychological environment and his right to feelings must be protected. Children will respond to empathy – to almost any adult who has that morale building quality of knowing how it is to be in their shoes. An empathic parent does not agree or disagree, but understands without judgment. Children reach out for understanding. Understanding helps to decrease the burden of worrying in isolation. "One of the patterns found in the homes of children with high self-esteem is a great deal of free and easy talk. Success in communication is important to self-respect." (Briggs)

"I-reactions"

> "I'm worried you'll be late for school."
> "I don't want to clean up these cookie crumbs on the floor!"
> "I can't count on your words when they don't match what you do."
> "I'm worried about your grades."
> "I like the dress you chose."

Parents would worry less if growth didn't follow "a switchback trail: three steps forward, two back, one around the bushes, and a few simply standing, before another forward leap". In some instances retreat may be necessary before the child has courage to venture into the unknown. For a reluctant child, structure new situations that will be guaranteed to provide success experiences. This will increase the likelihood that he will venture forth on his own initiative in the future.

When you repeatedly expect more than your child can do, your disappointments becomes the child's disappointment in himself. Knowing about the plan of growth gives guidelines for evaluating behavior and helps to reduce anxiety. One section of *Your Child's Self-Esteem* discusses the "Journey of Self" from birth through adolescence. Her helpful suggestions are concretized with specific examples. Later on in the book Briggs gives concrete suggestions and examples for handling negative feelings, anger, jealousy and discipline.

Remember: The perfect parent does not exist! Blaming yourself, your spouse, or the genetic endowment from in-laws does not help the child. All humans are in the process of becoming. Each move toward personal self-acceptance is an investment in the development of every member of the family. Since the past can not be changed, forget it! Start with the present and actively work toward helping your child like himself. The logo of tall trees surrounding the seedling was designed to emphasize the need for a nurturing environment to help our young ones grow.

"The greatest thing in the world is a human life. The greatest work in the world is a helpful touch upon that life."

Samoureux

CHILDREN AND PARENTS GARDENING TOGETHER

Encounters with nature provide the chance for a child to observe the miracle of life renewing itself from a seed. Hopefully, gardening will bring forth enthusiasm for appreciating the beauty in nature and create an awareness of the interdependence of all living things. It can also lead to an interest in nutrition, the preparation of food and scientific discoveries about plants.

A curious child may ask, "If we get our food from plants, where do plants get their food?" In the 17th and 18th centuries Jean van Helmont, Stephen Hales and Joseph Priestly performed experiments that revealed that plants make their own food from substances about them – soil, water, air and sunlight. "The leaves of green plants are actually 'food factories' where water, carbon dioxide from the air, and sunlight interact in a process called photosynthesis to make simple sugar that is the plant's food and at the same time releases life-sustaining oxygen into the air."

This helps a child to understand the interaction between plants and animals that is basic to ecology. Men and animals need plants to purify the air.

Successful projects for children require action and results. While waiting for the results from planted seeds you can discuss the action that is going on underground as plants exhibit their built-in response to light, water, gravity and touch. The mysterious force that causes plants to respond to a stimulus is known as tropism. Tropism experiments are easy to set up and observe at home. Radish and pole bean seeds are recommended because they germinate quickly. (They will germinate even faster when soaked in water overnight.)

Geotropism

A demonstration of a plant's movement in response to gravity will show a child what goes on underground. Make a clear plastic envelope using materials similar to a page from a photograph album. Cut three layers of paper toweling the size of the envelope and place inside. Saturate the paper toweling with water. Place the seeds in a straight row between the paper toweling and the plastic. Arrange the seeds a few inches from the edge and more than one inch apart. Hang the plastic envelope by a clothespin to a clothesline, curtain rod or something similar. In a few days your child will see the roots growing in a downward direction. As he turns the envelope up, down or sideways, (waiting a few days between each turn) your child can create a design as the roots continuously reach toward the earth. Children often like to make a design forming the first initial of their name. (Remember to keep the toweling moist with water.)

Hydrotropism

To illustrate a plant's movement in response to water you will need a clear plastic or glass container at least 8 inches long and 3 inches deep. Tape the drainage hole of a small clay flowerpot shut and fill with water only. Place it in one end of the container. Fill the rest of the glass or plastic container with soil that has been barely moistened with water. Plant melon seeds at the opposite end of the container up against the clear glass front. Now tape newspaper or foil around the edges so that no light can enter. When he peeks in a few days your child will observe that the roots are headed in the direction of the water filled clay pot. This ability to sense where water is helps plants to survive during periods of drought.

Phototropism

Bean seeds will exhibit a plant's response to light, not necessarily sunlight. Line a shoebox with aluminum foil and place two cups of gravel in the bottom. Add soil to within one inch from the top and dampen, but do not soak with water. At one end of the box cut out an inch of the cardboard from the top down. Plant the bean seeds and put the lid on the box. Place it on a windowsill and do not look for at least a week. When the child takes the lid off he will notice the bean plants bending toward the light at the end of the box.

To vary the experiment, place a small sweet potato in a glass of water at one end of the box. Insert a three quarter partition to one side of the box and another one to the other side of the box before putting the lid on. As the plant grows it will wind its way around the partitions toward the light.

Thigmotropism

Children love to impress their friends with this word. "Thigmo" comes from the Greek word for "touch" Some plants exhibit this tropism clearly by reaching out to grasp whatever comes close to them. Thigmotropism is a plant's version of Blind Man's Bluff. Pole beans and cucumbers will put on a highly dramatic show. As soon as the plants appear above the ground, sink short sticks into the ground to one side of each plant. When the second leaves have formed the plants will put out tendrils that latch onto, and curl around, the stick. Then the plant itself will twine round the stick. When this has occurred place a taller stick to the other side of each plant. The plant will shift its growth to the taller stick. If the experiment is done with several pots on window sills, the child can attach strings to the sticks and create a leafy arbor in his own bedroom. If there is insufficient light from the windows a small "grow light" can help to produce a harvest of beans.

Monsters

These same plants can become monsters in the outdoor garden.

They will attach themselves to other plants unless guided with turning and staking. Assign one child to defend the other plants from the "Cucumber Monster" as a means of keeping harmony in the garden.

"Nature never did betray the heart that loved her; 'tis her privilege through all the years of this life to lead from joy to joy,"

Wordsworth

Feature books and stories about Pat Nordberg

Never give up.

"The news I have for you is not good," the doctor's face was grim as he faced thirty-one-year-old Pat Nordberg. Her husband, Ode, gripped her hand. "Go on doctor," she said. "You have an aneurysm in the most inaccessible part of your brain. Your condition will get no better. You could die any time." *Page 177-184*

Crystal Cathedral Today - This is the monthly newsletter that carried an article about Pat.

Psalm 46
(Pat's Favorite Passage)

God is our refuge and strength,
a very present help in trouble.

Therefore we will not fear,
though the earth be removed,
and though the mountains be carried
into the midst of the sea.

God shall help her and that right early.

Be still, and know that I am God.

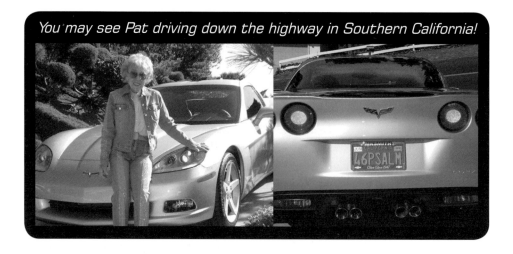

You may see Pat driving down the highway in Southern California!

HELPING
CHILDREN RECOVER

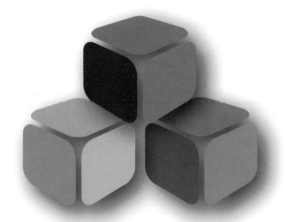

FROM LEARNING DISABILITIES
AND AUTISM

PATRICIA A. NORDBERG
MASTER OF SCIENCE IN SCHOOL PSYCHOLOGY

To order additional copies of
Helping Children Recover
Contact: Scott Company Publishing
P.O. Box 9707
Kalispell, MT 59904
Phone: 1-800-628-0212
Email: scott@scottcompany.net
$15.00 per single copy plus S&H

WWW.REACHINGFORHOPE.NET

Scott Company Publishing
Kalispell, Montana
1-800-628-0212
scott@scottcompany.net

Learning Disabilities Association *of America*

Since 1963, LDA has provided support to people with learning disabilities, their parents, teachers and other professionals. At the national, state and local levels, LDA provides cutting edge information on learning disabilities, practical solutions, and a comprehensive network of resources. These services make the Learning Disabilities Association of America the leading resource for information on learning disabilities.

Learning Disabilities Association of America
4156 Library Road • Pittsburgh, PA 15234-1349
Phone (412) 341-1515 Fax (412) 344-0224
www.ldanatl.org

Find the LDA Near You

You are not alone. LDA has state and/or local affiliates in every state. Membership in LDA includes membership in your state and local affiliate, giving you access to an array of services and supports.

State and local affiliates offer a variety of services that can make a difference in the lives of individuals with learning disabilities and their families. State and local activities may include: support groups, regular informational meetings, resource libraries, advocacy assistance, newsletters, annual conferences and opportunities to network with other parents, teachers, professionals and adults.

LDA-CA State Office
808 West Balboa Blvd.
Newport Beach, CA 92661
Phone: (949) 673-3612
Email: ca-lda@sbcglobal.net

LDA-CA Local Affiliates

East Bay
P.O. Box 5513
Berkeley, CA 94705
Phone: 510-433-7934
www.EastBayLDA.org

Pomona Valley
PO Box 1114
Claremont, CA 91711
Phone: 909-621-1494
Email: PVLDA@aol.com

San Diego
P.O. Box 421111
San Diego, CA 92142
Phone: 858-467-9158
www.LDASanDiego.org

Los Angeles
P.O. Box 1067
Sierra Madre, CA 91025
Phone: 626-355-0240
Email: lalda@verizon.net

Orange County
P.O. Box 25772
Santa Ana, CA 92799-5772
Phone: 714-547-4206
www.oclda.org